SCHRIFTENREIHE DES IMT 5

Schriftenreihe des Instituts für
Management und Tourismus

Herausgegeben von Christian Eilzer,
Bernd Eisenstein und Wolfgang Georg Arlt

Christian Eilzer,
Wolfgang Georg Arlt,
Bernd Eisenstein (Eds.)

Global Experiences
in Tourism

Proceedings of the International
Competence Network of
Tourism Management (ICNT)

Martin Meidenbauer »

Christian Eilzer, Studium International Tourism Management
(Master of Arts), BWL-Studium (Dipl.-Kfm. FH), Projekttätigkeit
für die inspektour GmbH, von 2004 bis 2006 wissenschaftlicher
Mitarbeiter im Studiengang International Tourism Management
an der FH Westküste, ab 2006 an der Hochschule Mitarbeiter
im Institut für Management und Tourismus sowie seit 2009
Fachbereichsgeschäftsführer des Fachbereichs Wirtschaft der
FH Westküste.

Dr. Bernd Eisenstein, Dipl.-Kaufmann und Dipl.-Geograph,
Dr. phil. (Universität Trier); zahlreiche Beratungs- und Gutachter-
tätigkeiten im Tourismus. Seit 1997 Professor für Tourismusmanagement, seit 2006 Leiter des Instituts für Management
und Tourismus (IMT) der FH Westküste.

Dr. Wolfgang Georg Arlt FRGS, Studium der Sinologie, Soziologie
und Politologie an der FU Berlin (M.A. und Dr. rer. pol.). Studienauf-
enthalte in Taiwan und Hong Kong. Seit 2002 Professor für Internatio-
nales Tourismusmanagement, seit 2007 an der FH Westküste.
Gastprofessor an Universitäten in China und Großbritannien, Fellow
of the Royal Geographical Society. Leiter des COTRI China Outbound
Tourism Research Institute.

Bibliografische Information der Deutschen
Nationalbibliothek
Die Deutsche Nationalbibliothek verzeichnet
diese Publikation in der Deutschen
Nationalbibliografie; detaillierte
bibliografische Daten sind im Internet
über http://dnb.d-nb.de abrufbar.

© 2011 Martin Meidenbauer
Verlagsbuchhandlung, München

Printed in Germany

Gedruckt auf chlorfrei gebleichtem,
säurefreiem und alterungsbeständigem
Papier (ISO 9706)

ISBN 978-3-89975-253-3
Verlagsverzeichnis schickt gern:
Martin Meidenbauer Verlagsbuchhandlung
Schwanthalerstr. 81
D-80336 München

www.m-verlag.net

Foreword

Tourism encompasses increasingly different concepts of human behavior. A visit to Dubai Airport Terminal 3 at two o'clock in the morning will present a sample of all kind of travelers: Voluptuous black ladies from the US in tight pants walking close to a Saudi-Arabian women looking out through the narrow slit of her niqab, Chinese businessmen in western suit searching for their boarding gate passing a couple of German backpackers on their honeymoon trip. Orthodox Jewish diamond dealers with peyes sideburns from Holland sit next to bored Indian software experts plugging their tablet computer into the socket at the side of the Starbucks for recharging, as further down the central shopping mall giggling members of the Malayan female national Badminton team meet spoilt rich South African kids looking at the latest gadgets in the electronics duty free store on their way back to school in the UK.

Dubai Terminal 3, the biggest airport terminal in the world, seems to be the perfect illustration of what Marc Augé, the French anthropologist, had in mind when he published in 1995 his seminal book about non-places, localities so detached from their geographical reality that they could be anywhere. Only when the public announcement system five times a day starts to transmit the calling of the muezzin, travelers are reminded of the location of their transit point.

The business lounge adds as local flavor Arab bread alongside Italian pasta and French champagne, but for the visitors checking their Blackberries that hardly matters. This is certainly the meeting place for those who Pico Iyer, the famous Indian-British philosopher of travelling, recently described in an article in *Time Magazine* as *aerotropolitans*, who have more in common with the person slumbering on the adjacent sofa than with their neighbors in their seldom-visited apartment in what they will have to identify on their visa application as home country.

What brings all these weary, exited or bored passengers here is not the attractiveness of the destination Dubai but the hub-and-spoke system of Emirates Airlines. With its peculiar combination of private and government involvement, not to be found in any textbook of macroeconomics, low prices and globalised services it has developed into an airline making more profit than all American airlines combined. Public announcements in at least three languages naming the dozen or more languages spoken by the stewardesses on board will soon interrupt the

5

eagerly started entertainment of choice in the aircraft, one of 1,500 music and movie programs available even in Economy class.

Tourism, we said above, encompasses more and more different concepts of human behavior. Some authors have proposed abolishing the entire concept: Hall and Urry favor the term *Mobility*, Zhang Lingyun developed the concept of *Unusual Environment existence*, which would put Iyers *aerotropolitans*, British pensioners regularly travelling to their second home in Spain and the Hong Kong-based professor spending every weekend in Shenzhen in the same category as the multi-lingual Emirates stewardesses and therefore outside of the definition of tourists. However, regardless of how it is called and conceptualized, tourism will continue to be integrated more and more into the experience of the majority of the inhabitants of our planet.

This book brings together texts from tourism experts from a number of countries and continents. Published in Germany but based on the input from two conferences of the International Competence Network of Tourism (ICNT) in Mexico and South Africa, it reflects the variety of topics and issues in today's global tourism and the different ways of addressing them. Quantitative studies for instance on travel behavior and destination images are sitting next to qualitative studies on internet usage and culture tourism; modern developments show their positive potential for instance in using special forms of GIS in Iceland but also their destructive force for instance in the mix-up of traditional festivals with commerce-driven globalized *Ersatz*-culture as in the case of the fight between the *Día de Los Muertos* and *Halloween* in Mexico.

Wolfgang Georg Arlt

Index

Cultural Tourism in Northeast Iceland: Creating new Opportunities through community-based Strategic Planning

John S. Hull, Michael Lück, Edward H. Huijbens

Abstract

Cultural tourism has continued to grow over the past decades, and is increasingly recognized as a tool for regional and community development. The rich cultural heritage of Iceland is identified as an important asset by tourism policymakers to diversify destination offerings that are primarily focused on nature-based products. The Regional Development Agency in Northeast Iceland, in an effort to integrate cultural offerings into their attractions and activities, have identified a range of tangible and intangible cultural and historic resources that are valuable for the strengthening of tourism development in the region. These resources include lighthouses, archaeological sites, cultural monuments, cultural events and folk tales. This paper reports on the implementation of a participatory planning strategy, PAGIS (Participatory Approach Using Geographical Information Systems), as a tool for strategic planning and development. Such mapping assists planners and policymakers in the development of tourism spaces, as well as tourists in navigating their holiday destination. In consultation with various local stakeholders, and the collaboration with external organizations, such as the Christmas Cities Network, a strategic tourism plan for Northeast Iceland was developed, linking a series of resource clusters (cuisine, folklore, lighthouses) in the region using geographic information systems (GIS).

1. Introduction

Over the last four decades, tourism policymakers acknowledge that cultural tourism has evolved into a distinct niche market that has continued to grow in importance as travelers seek a greater appreciation of cultural heritage assets and their associated experiences and products at destinations (McKercher & du Cros, 2002). At the beginning of the 21st century, the United Nations World Tourism Organisation reports that 37% of all international trips include a cultural component and that cultural tourism is growing at 15% annually (UNWTO, 2008). In Europe, the ATLAS cultural tourism survey reports that the proportion of tourists on a cultural holiday has increased from 17% in 1997 to 31% in 2007 (ATLAS, 2008).

For Iceland, these cultural assets are linked to a medieval Norse heritage that began with the settlement of the island about 870 AD as part of a larger westward expansion and exploration of the North Atlantic at the time. The majority of early settlers arrived from the west coast of Norway, as well as Norse communities in Ireland and Great Britain (Kellogg, 2001). As Kellogg (2001, p. xv) notes,

….the mention of medieval Norseman summons images of pagan Vikings, in beautiful, far-sailing ships, who for two hundred years terrified the peaceful coasts of France and the British Isles…. The Norseman were not merely Viking marauders, however. A people of great organizational genius and maritime skill, they were traders, explorers, settlers, landowners, and on an increasingly large scale, able political leaders.

In the late Middle Ages, these settlers were part of a time of innovation in literature in Europe. In the thirteenth and fourteenth centuries about forty works of historical fiction, the Icelandic Sagas, were completed documenting early settlement in Iceland and events of the larger Norse world (Kellogg, 2001). The Icelandic Sagas are recognized at the crowning achievement of medieval narrative art in Scandinavia (Kellogg, 2001) and describe

an agricultural world where leisure was at a premium. The sagas… are full of work. The action takes place in a context of sheep-herding, horse-breeding, weaving, cooking, washing, building, clearing land and expanding holdings, trading by ship with mainland Europe and the British Isles (Smiley, 2001, p. xi).

The sagas are the basis for a rich cultural heritage that is attracting an increasing number of visitors to Iceland. The Icelandic Tourism Board reports that culture and history is the second most important trip motivator for non-resident visitors (ITB, 2005).

In 2008, over 502,000 international tourists visited Iceland with over 80% of first time visitors mainly from Europe and North America (ITB, 2009). Tourism is identified as the third largest foreign currency earner for the Icelandic economy with 2006 total tourism receipts measured at 70,6 billion Icelandic Krónur (appr. $US 0.56 billion), with 5,2 billion spent directly on culture and recreation. The sector contributed on average 4.6% to the nation's GDP in the period 2000-2006, providing almost 20% of the country's income from foreign sources in 2006 (Statistics Iceland, 2008).

In this context this paper examines the present development of cultural tourism in Northeast Iceland and the growing significance of the area's cultural heritage assets as part of a new five-year strategic plan for the region completed in 2008 (Hull, Patterson, Huijbens & Milne, 2008b). In the second section, there is a review of definitions and the methodology while in the third section an inventory of the cultural heritage assets (tangible and intangible) in the region is summarized. The fourth section outlines present efforts to integrate these assets into new tourist products and experiences to attract the "cultural" tourist to the region.

2.   Defining Cultural Tourism Using PAGIS

"Cultural" refers to the complex blend of shared values, customs, languages, artefacts, and experiences that characterize a society (Government of Newfoundland and Labrador, 2006). Drawing on these aspects, cultural tourism is basically defined as special interest travel ranging from the examination of physical remains of past and natural landscapes to the experience of local cultural traditions (Timothy & Boyd, 2003; Richards, 2001; Zeppel & Hall, 1992). In utilizing the term cultural tourism both the cultural nature of, and the role of, tourism as a process and a set of practices that revolve around the behavioural pragmatics of societies, and the learning and transmission of meanings through symbols embodied through objects, are explicitly acknowleded (Robinson & Smith, 2006).

11

UNESCO (2009) categorises cultural heritage into two main categories – tangible (objects) and intangible (symbols). Tangible heritage represents the physical artifacts of past cultures and civilizations represented by various forms of landscapes, architecture, artifacts, and art while intangible cultural heritage consists of non-physical characteristics, practices, representations, expressions, as well as knowledge and skills that identify and define a group or civilization. These intangible characteristics are manifested through oral traditions, music, dance, drama, social practices, knowledge practices, and traditional crafts-manship. The summary of the cultural heritage of Northeast Iceland to be presented here has been categorized according to these two groupings using PAGIS (Participatory Approach Using Geographical Information Systems), a method to facilitate community-based tourism planning (Hasse & Milne, 2005).

The principal idea of PAGIS is to integrate local knowledge, such as values, emotions and perceptions of a place that have been gathered in participatory mapping exercises, into GIS. This local knowledge includes the narratives of local people and reflects the diverse range of opinions of particular places in the community. (Hasse & Milne, 2005, p. 277).

Building community capacity is acknowledged as critical element to ensure success for new tourism development in peripheral regions (Moscardo, 2008). In the context of Northeast Iceland, over sixty maps were generated in cooperation with local residents to identify the natural and cultural heritage, socio-economic conditions, and tourism products and services in the region. The maps assisted in establishing a baseline for tourism planning (Hull, Patterson, Huijbens & Milne, 2008a). The maps also provided an understanding of the needs and resource assets of the destination, which is recognized as a critical first step in developing new tourism products (Fennell, 2002).

Eight public consultations were organised using the maps to identify strategic priorities for development and solicit feedback. In addition, in-depth interviews with twenty key stakeholders were completed to verify the results of the public consultations and to further identify opportunities and needs for the tourism industry. Secondary research also included a review of government reports, academic literature, and web-based information. These data generated a list of priorities and strategic recommendations for tourism development (Hull et al., 2008b).

3. Tangible and Intangible Cultural Heritage

Northeast Iceland is Iceland's largest Administrative District, with a land area of approximately 18,439 square kilometers comprising 18.32% of terrestrial Iceland (Atthing, 2009) (Figure 1).

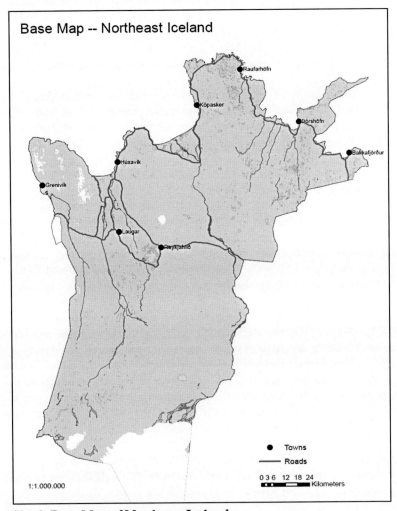

Fig. 1: Base Map of Northeast Iceland

3.1 Tangible Heritage

Historically, Northeast Iceland's cultural heritage has been largely dependent on links to marine and agricultural resources in the region. Throughout Iceland's history sea-faring and fisheries have played a large part in people's subsistence along with sheep rearing, both conducted in harsh semi-polar environments. Some efforts have been made in pointing to this as a resource in cultural tourism development. In Northeast Iceland, the Northern Coastal Experience project (NORCE, 2009) provides one example of the efforts in the region to link culture and tourism.

For the majority of residents, their livelihoods have depended upon the abundant marine resources. Seventy five percent of all Iceland's merchandise exports are derived from marine products (UNESCO, 2009). The increasing importance of these resources for tourism reflects a resurgence in cultural identity and increased local pride as is represented by the cultural centres, lighthouses, archaeological sites and cultural monuments being made visitable (Dicks, 2004) in the region.

The cultural centres in the towns of Húsavík, Kelduhverfi, Kópasker, Raufarhöfn, Þórshöfn and Bakkafjörður are predominantly focused on coastal histories and illustrate the daily life and occupation of the regions' inhabitants in times past (Atthing, 2009). Maritime themed cultural centres include the Húsavík Whale Museum and the Húsavík's Museum of Natural History which display not only artefacts of whales but also exhibits on local events and sea-faring equipment. These museums also provide an educational component to the whale watching trips offered in the area during the summer months. In conjunction with the regional cultural centres are food festivals and sightseeing tours that create a cluster of attractions and activities for visitors.

A key example speaking to the importance of the historical dependence on the marine resources and the sea is the mapped network of lighthouses. Tour operators are now including visits to lighthouses in their tours as international interest in lighthouses grows through new products linked to touring and accommodation (Inn and Around, 2009; Norwegian Lighthouse Association, 2009). One such tour in Northeast Iceland is to the site of Flateyjarviti located on the highest point on the Island of Flatey ("Flat Island") in Skjálfandi Bay (Figure 2).

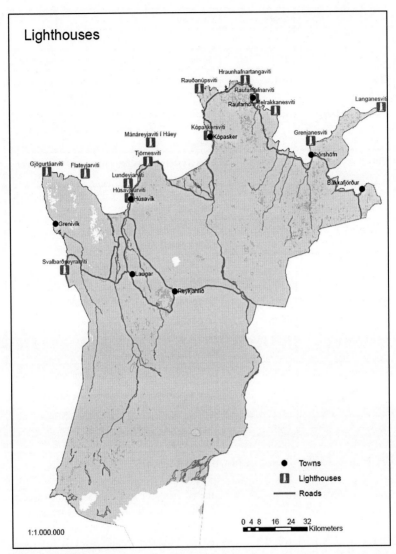

Fig. 2: Lighthouses

Name	Year	Location
Flatey (2)	1963, Est. 1913	On the highest point of Flatey island
Gjögurtá	1970	On the east side of the entrance to the Eyjafjörður
Grenjanes	1945	On a cape at the east entrance to the Lónafjörður, north of the fishing town of Þórshöfn
Hraunhafnartangi	1951	Iceland's northernmost lighthouse, standing south of the Arctic Circle at the north-eastern tip of the island
Húsavík	Unknown	On a promontory on the north side of the entrance to Húsavík harbor
Kópasker (Grímshafnartangi)	1951	On a promontory on the north side of the entrance to the harbor of Kópasker
Langanes (2)	1950, Est. 1914	The lighthouse marks the end of Fontur, a long, narrow peninsula
Lundey	1977	The lantern can be seen toward the left end of the Lundey island in a view from the sea
Mánáreyjar	1982	On the highest point of the Mánáreyjar island
Melrakkanes	1956	On a cape southeast of Raufarhöfn
Rauðinúpur (2)	1958, Est. 1929	On a promontory at the northwestern corner of the Melrakkaslétta
Raufarhöfn	1920	On the shore, north of Svalbarðseyri village
Raufarhöfn	1931	On the south side of the entrance to Raufarhöfn harbor
Tjörnes	1929	The lighthouse marks a prominent cape on the north coast

Key Fig. 2: Lighthouses in Northeast Iceland

Archaeological sites provide evidence of first settlers to Iceland; to many visitors this is of most interest when it comes to Icelandic culture. The Swedish explorer, Garðar Svavarsson, was the first man to discover that Iceland was an island. He wintered in Húsavík four years before the arrival of Ingólfur Arnarson, the first official settler in Iceland. A large number of settlers from the region are identified in Landnáma, the book of settlements, and many burial mounds of the first Þingeyjarsýsla settlers have been found (Atthing, 2008).

16

About the year 963, the descendants of the settlers decided to convene their district assembly (þing) at Þingey island in Skjálfandafljót. This assembly is referred to several times in written sources during the period of approximately 950–1250 (Atthing, 2009). Many of the ruins connected with the assembly (þing) are still visible in the municipality of Þingeyjarsveit and there are several sites like Baldursheimur and Grímsstaðir in the Mývatnssveit (Mývatn area) (Figure 3).

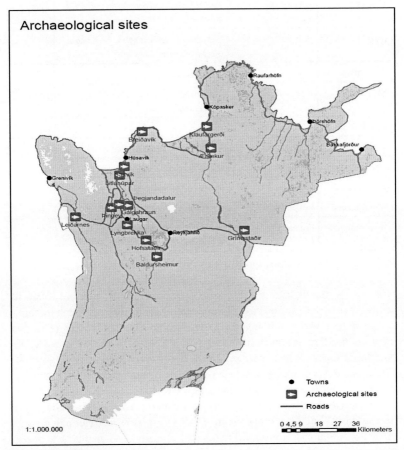

Fig. 3: Archaeological Sites

Archaeological Sites			
Location	**Site**	**What is it**	**Visibility**
Aðaldal	Þegjandadalur	Fornminjar	Ruins
Aðaldal	Litlu-Núpar	Pagan graves, one containing the remnants of a boat	
Mývatnssveit	Baldursheimur	Pagan grave	Farm
Mývatnssveit	Grímsstaðir	Pagan grave, one containing remains of a horse	Farm
Mývatnssveit	Hofsstaðir	Old houses, was thought to be a pagan temple but most likely isn't	
Norðurþingi	Saltvík	Pagan grave	Farm
Norðurþingi	Kuml á Ærlæk	Woman jewellery, on exhibition in the National Museum	Farm
Norðurþingi	Kuml í Klaufagerði	Pagan grave	Farm
Þingeyjarsveit	Þingey	Ruins, connected to the assembly	
Þingeyjarsveit	Skuldaþingsey	Ruins, connected to the assembly	
Þingeyjarsveit	Leiðarnes	Ruins, connected to the assembly	
Þingeyjarsveit	Lyngbrekka	Pagan grave	Farm
Tjörneshreppur	Breiðavík	Ruins of houses from the period of settlement	Farm

Key Fig. 3: Archaeological Sites in Northeast Iceland

Sites of archeological interest often coincide with sites of historic importance or great interest. These sites tell stories of the hardships involved in making a living on a semi-polar island, through centuries prior to modernization, which came in the mid twentieth century. In Northeast Iceland there are many of these cultural monuments (Figure 4). There are several well-preserved buildings being refurbished including the traditional Icelandic turfhouse and a Christian church (built in 1865) which overlooks the delta of the Fnjóská River in Laufás. The oldest part of the farm building dates from 1840. It is now a regional history museum containing household items and utensils used at the start of the 20th century and remains as an excellent example of a typical farmhouse of the period (Hull et al., 2008a).

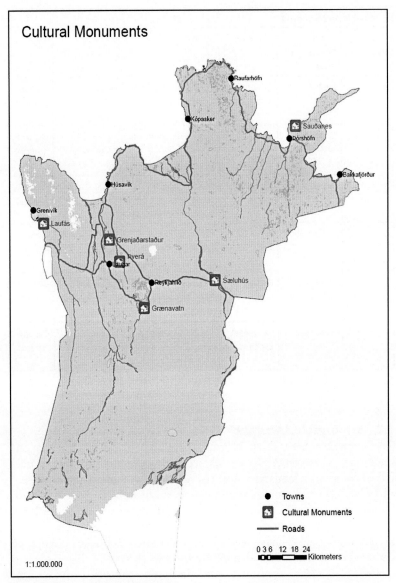

Fig. 4: Cultural Monuments

Cultural Monument Sites

Tourism Region	Cultural Monument Sites	Location	What is it	Visibility	Type
1	Laufás	Grýtubak-kahreppi	Turf house, museum, vicarage	House, information signs	Cultural history
1	Grenjaðar-staður	Aðaldal	Turf house, museum, vicarage	A house, an information sign	Cultural history
1	Þverá	Þingey-jarsveit	Turf house, turf stables, belongs to the National museum	Houses, signs	Cultural remains
5	Grænavatn	Mývatnss-veit	Old timber house, belongs to the National museum	A house and a sign	Cultural history
5	Jökulsá á fjöllum	Norðurþing	Rest house from 1880, belongs to the National museum	House and signs	Cultural history
2	Sauðanes	Langanes-byggð	The old vicarage, an exhibition, belongs to the National museum	House, information signs	Cultural remains

Key Fig. 4: Cultural Monument Sites in Northeast Iceland

3.2 Intangible Heritage

The intangible heritage of Northeast Iceland is focused on religious traditions, gastronomy, events, folklore, and traditional farming practices linked to specific landscape features and communities. The conversion of Iceland to Christianity was a unique event in Icelandic history and an important part of the country's culture and identity. In the year 1000, Iceland was on the brink of civil war. The nation was deeply divided between different religious factions so it was decreed by the Althing, the parliament, at Þingvellir, that all Icelanders should be baptized into Christianity, and as a result the whole society literally abandoned its ancient heathen beliefs.

This history is behind the naming of one of Northeast Iceland's most spectacular natural attractions - the Goðafoss (Waterfall of the Gods). The actual waterfall is located in Northeast Iceland in the Skjálfandfljót River. The Law Speaker of Althing - Þorgeir, decided to lead by example in renouncing his heathen beliefs and took all of his Norse gods idols to the Skjálfandafljót River and threw them over the great waterfall – know ever since as the Goðafoss Waterfall (Atthing, 2008).

Strong traditions in food have been fostered from a long history of fishing and farming. Seafood and lamb are the main source of food products although trout/salmon from the freshwater lakes also feature in traditional food fare. Visitors to Mývatn are often treated to a local speciality – Hverabrauð (steam bread), a sweet rye bread made with molasses and cooked in an underground earth oven heated by geo-thermal steam.

Events and festivals offer visitors the opportunity to experience local culture. Most festivals are small, local community events featuring maritime and agricultural themes. The July 'Days of Joy' Summer Festival in Þórshöfn is an example of an annual family weekend festival. Included in the festival activities are a fishing contest, local artist's exhibition, fitness contest, and markets offering local fish and meat products (Langanesbyggd, 2009) (Figure 5).

Cultural Events and Festivals			
No.	Event	Location	Date	Notes
1	Folaldasýning	Norðurþing	Jan-Feb	Foal exhibition and competition
2	Aðventudagskrá	Mývatnssveit	Nov-Dec (advent)	Advent programme centred on the Yule lads, traditional foodmaking
2	Ísmót	Mývatnssveit	Feb-Mar	Horse sports on ice
2	Kóramót	Mývatnssveit	June	National choir competition
2	Páskadagskrá Hótel Reynihlíð	Mývatnssveit	Easter (March-April)	Easter programme, concerts/activities
2	Píslargangan	Mývatnssveit	Good Friday	36 km walk around lake on Good Friday

3	Hátíðahöld á 17. júní	Þórshöfn	17th June	Independence Day parade, signing
3	Ísmót	Langanes	Feb-Mar	Horse sports on ice
3	Kátir dagar	Þórshöfn	July	4 day town festival with concerts, activities
3	Sjómannadagshátíð	Þórshöfn	June	Fisherman´s festival and seabird egg day
4	Vortónleikar karlakórsins Hreims	Aðaldalur	March-April	Annual concert of regional man´s choir
5	Einarstaðamótið	Einarstaðir, Þingeyjarsveit	August	Weekend tournament of horse sports
6	Hátíðahöld á 17. júní	Húsavík	17th June	Independence Day parade, signing
6	Mærudagar	Húsavík	July	Week long town festival
6	Sjómannadagshátíð	Húsavík	June	Fisherman´s festival
7	Hátíðahöld á 17. júní	Kópasker og Öxarfjörður	17th June	Independence Day parade, signing
7	Menningar- og markaðsdagur	Kópasker	1st Weekend December	Culture and market day, music and more
8	Sléttuganga	Melrakkaslétta	July	30 km walk and dinner
9	Bjart er yfir Raufarhöfn	Raufarhöfn	October	Days of culture, music, handicrafts
9	Hátíðahöld á 17. júní	Raufarhöfn	17th June	Independence Day parade, signing
9	Hrútadagur	Raufarhöfn	October	Male sheep day. Soup making
9	Sjómannadagshátíð	Raufarhöfn	June	Fisherman´s Festival
10	Jökulsárhlau	Jökulsárgljúfur National Park	July	Long distance race in National Park

Key Fig. 5: Cultural Events and Festivals in Northeast Iceland

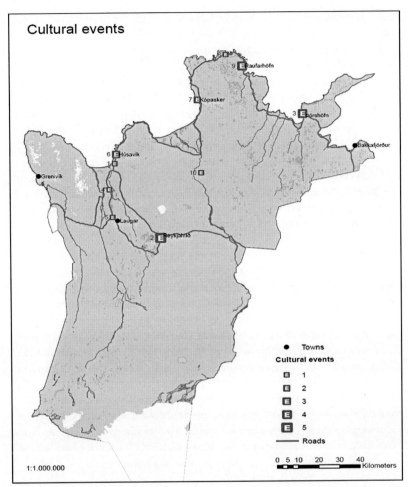

Fig. 5: Cultural Events

Northeast Iceland also has its own renditions of Icelandic folklore, especially tales of encounters with The Yule Lads, Trolls, Gods and Saga characters linked to the unique features of the landscape (Figure 6). When the snows come, the thirteen Yule Lads, who live in the Dimmuborgir lava fields of Mývatnssveit appear for the Christmas Yuletide season. A program called Magical Mývatn - Yuletide wonderland features the Yule Lads and includes the folklore/traditions such as the Christmas annual bath at Mývatn Nature Baths.

A driving tour of Northeast Iceland provides tourists with opportunities to see the evidence of the tale "The Night Troll and her Boat at Mývatn". A story is told of a troll-wife who did the Mývatn folk great harm by stealing their fish from Lake Mývatn under the cloak of darkness. One night she was late returning home to the Highlands and when the sun came up she was forced to put down her boat and climb in, but alas both turned to stone as Icelandic night trolls do once hit by the first rays of the morning sun. The evidence of the Troll-wife's nökkvi (boat) can be found on a slope known as Nökkvabrekka, about halfway between Mývatn and Skessuhali. It is said there are still signs of oars and rowlocks even a pile of rock in the stern which are believed to be the troll-wife's last resting place (Hjalmarsson, 2000).

Although not quite as mythical, the Icelandic Sagas also provide for stories narrating the landscape. In the Saga of Grettir the Strong, the story tells how outlaw Grettir Ásmundarson, while hiding out at the farm of Sandhaugar in Bárðardalur volunteered to stay and guard the place while the rest of the household went to Mass for Christmas. This was a very brave act as the men left behind to guard the farm during the last two Christmases had disappeared. In the middle of night there was a commotion and Grettir was confronted with a fearsome troll-wife. They fought until Grettir finally threw the troll into the river canyon and the waterfall Goðafoss. Grettir believed that there were more trolls in the river canyon and came back to explore the caves behind the waterfall with the aid of the local priest. After a mighty battle with a fearsome giant who guarded the caves, Grettir discovered a great deal of treasure but more important to him was taking back the bones of the two other watchmen of the farm he found so they could be properly buried (Viking Age Classics, 1997).

Ásbyrgi, a 3,5 km long canyon part of Vatnajkoull National Park, provides another the setting for a tale located in Northeast Iceland, this time relating to the old pagan gods from before Icelanders adopted Christianity. According to folklore, Óðinn the highest of the Norse gods was riding through the heavens one day but was momentarily distracted and came a little too close to the earth. Óðinn's actions caused Sleipnir his mighty eight legged stead to briefly touch the ground with one of its hoofs thus forming the Ásbyrgi canyon. In the middle of the canyon there is "The Island", a free standing rock which is shaped like a horseshoe and it is said to be Sleipnir's Hoofprint (Hjalmarsson, 2000).

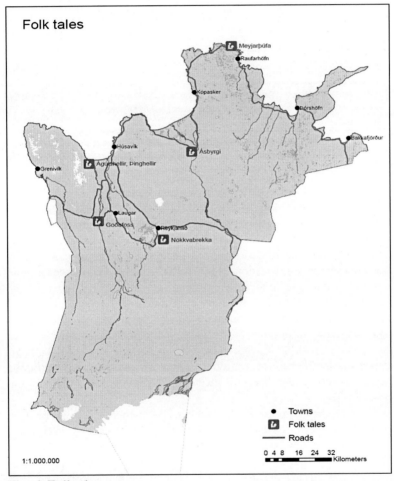

Fig. 6: Folktales

John S. Hull, Michael Lück, Edward H. Huijbens

Folklore - Tales			
Location	Site	What is it	Visibility
Norðurþingi	Meyjarþúfa	Tussock connected with a story about the origin of people living in the area	Tussock
Þingeyjarsveit	Ágúlshellir, Þinghellir	Cave, home of the giant Ágúll	Cave
Goðafoss	Waterfall of the Gods (Goðafoss)	Goðafoss waterfall and caves	Waterfall & caves
Nökkvabrekka, (halfway between Mývatn and Skessuhali)	The Night Troll and her Boat at Mývatn	Nökkvabrekka (boat-slope) on Skessuhali (Troll-wife's Ridge)	A rock in the shape of a boat
Ásbyrgi	Ásbyrgi: Sleipnir's Hoofprint	"The Island", a free standing rock which is shaped like a horseshoe	Horseshoe shaped rock

Key Fig. 6: Folklore – Tales in Northeast Iceland

Finally, in Northeast Iceland, visitors have the opportunity to engage in agritourism activities through the network of Icelandic farm holiday accommodations in the region, experiencing modern day farming and its historic roots in a live setting. Many of the region's events focus around both seasonal and traditional farming practices. The réttir (sheep gathering) in the autumn offer much to enrich the region's landscape and provide visitors with an opportunity to gain an insight into the history and ongoing importance of traditional agricultural practices to communities such as Mývatn, where sheep farming has been the most important livelihood for centuries. There are many sheep gathering places in Northeast Iceland including Mýrarrétt, Sellandarétt, and Strengjarétt.

Through the inventory of the tangible and intangible cultural heritage elements in Northeast Iceland, public and private tourism stakeholders are developing new tourism products and packages that will appeal to the cultural tourist. Cultural heritage places are an important part of the tourism mix of any destination and must be known beyond the local heritage community; provide experiences that can be consumed; be interesting and unique; absorb visitation; and be accessible (McKercher & du Cros, 2002; Richards, 1996). The five-year plan for tourism in

Northeast Iceland summarized in the next section provides recommendations on the cultural heritage assets that have the greatest capacity to provide a compelling reason to visit the region (Hull et al., 2008b).

4. Efforts to Attract Cultural Tourists

In an effort to better manage tourism's growth in Northeast Iceland, the Regional Development Agency commissioned a tourism strategy to outline a direction for future planning and development from 2009 to 2014 (Hull et al., 2008b), based on the above outlined inventory and mapping of resources. As part of the vision for tourism, it was argued by residents in the public consultation meetings that marketing, product development, support services, education and training, access and infrastructure development must occur simultaneously in order to build a quality product throughout the region to support the principles of sustainable tourism (Figure 7).

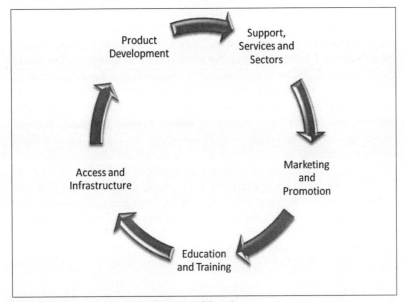

Fig. 7: Efforts to Attract Cultural Tourists

In addressing cultural tourism products, the region is focusing on developing activities and programs linked to agritourism and maritime heritage. A group of eighteen local companies have formed a cluster around the development of local food and food production in partnership with the farmstay accommodations and farms in the region. There are over 245 farms primarily herding sheep, but also cattle, pigs and chickens. Even though commercial fishing has decreased overtime with the decline in marine resources, two aquaculture sites produce salmon and trout while another is experimenting with halibut, turbot, and other small species. The abundant local trout populations have historically led to the development of a regional cuisine featuring smoked trout. At present there is a movement towards the development of regional cuisine using locally cultivated products and the International Culinary Tourism Association reports that cuisine is not only one of the top three favourite tourism activities but is also satisfying a growing tourist demand for more interactive, hands-on experiences (Hull & Palsson, 2009; International Culinary Tourism Association, 2009).

Another new product being developed is linked to the Yulelads at Mývatn where the regional development agency, funded by the European Union's Northern Periphery Programme developed the concept working with partners in Finland and Sweden (Snow Magic, 2009) and the Christmas Cities Network (2009) to design and promote attractive products, services and events based on the sustainable use of snow and ice. The overall aim is to support tourist activities and local society through the use of new technologies, local resources, legends and folklore and winter time traditions linked to the Icelandic Yuletide season to expand the winter tourism market in the region (Snow Magic, 2009).

Finally, a number of local residents have proposed the development of a Lighthouse Trail for visitors traveling along the coast of Northeast Iceland. One of the ideas is to create a Lighthouses and Legends tour through the region as a way to link tangible and intangible cultural resources that will attract travelers that have formed networks and associations interested in lighthouses (Figure 8).

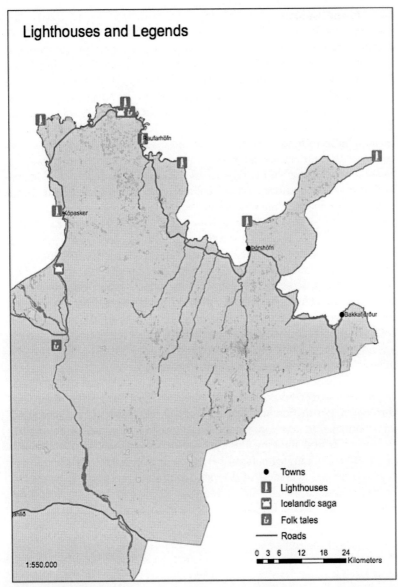

Fig. 8: Lighthouses

5. Conclusions

Globally, cultural heritage sites are viewed by governments and destinations as a major part of the economic development process (Timothy & Boyd, 2003; McKercher & du Cros, 2002). These sites assist in promoting local community interest in a regions' history as well as encouraging visitors to stay longer in the region. In Northeast Iceland, a newly launched five year strategic tourism plan by the regional development agency using PAGIS (participatory approaches to geographic information systems) has increased resident awareness and pride in the cultural heritage of the region through the mapping of tangible and intangible heritage assets. Through community workshops and surveys, a number of new cultural tourism products have been identified to diversify the regional economy.

Moscardo (2008) argues that one of the greatest barriers to the effective use of tourism as a development strategy has been inadequate attention to building community capacity and readiness for development. Improving community knowledge and participation in the tourism development process are identified as important in ensuring successful development. Through the use of PAGIS, local residents have been directly involved in the planning process as part of the mapping of tourism assets and in determining priorities for development which they are now implementing through a series of product development clusters linked to cuisine, folklore, and lighthouses.

Mapping assists planners and policymakers not only in the production of tourism spaces but also serves to assist visitors in guiding their way through a destination and learning about its histories, cultures, and environments. In addition, mapping supports the documentation of sites to inform critical thinking and decision-making (Hanna & Del Casino, 2003). The mapping of cultural heritage assets in Northeast Iceland has fostered greater awareness of the value of these assets to the region. One of the major challenges facing local residents will be how well they conserve and manage these assets for tourism consumption to promote the long-term sustainability of the industry.

References

ATLAS (2008). *From Cultural to Creative Tourism.* Retrieved November 15, 2008 from http://www.atlas-euro.org/

Atthing (2008). *2008 Northeast Iceland Guidebook.* Húsavík, Iceland: Atthing.

Atthing (2009). *Visit Northeast Iceland.* Retrieved February 22, 2009, from http://www.visitnortheasticeland.is/

Christmas Cities Nework (2009). *Welcome to the Christmas Cities Network.* Retrieved April 26, 2009, from http://www.christmas-cities.net/about_us.html

Dicks, B. (2004). *Culture on Display. The Production of Contemporary Visitability.* Maidenhead, UK: Open University Press.

Fennell, D. (2002). *Ecotourism Programme Planning.* Wallingford, UK: CABI Publishing.

Government of Newfoundland and Labrador (2006). *Creative Newfoundland and Labrador: The Blueprint for Development and Investment in Culture.* St. John's NL: Government of Newfoundland and Labrador, Canada.

Hanna, S. & Del Casino, V.J. (2003). Introduction: tourism spaces, mapped representations, and the practices of identity. In S. Hanna & V.J. Del Casino (Eds.) *Mapping tourism* (pp. 1-27). Minneapolis MN, USA: University of Minnesota Press.

Hasse, J. & S.S. Milne (2005). Participatory approaches and geographical information systems (PAGIS) in tourism planning. *Tourism Geographies, 7*(3), 272-289.

Hjalmarsson, J.R. (2000). *A Travelers Guide to Icelandic Folk Tales.* Huntingdon UK: Edda UK Ltd.

Hull, J.S. & Palsson, A-P. (2009). Koillis – Islanti: Northeast Iceland Culinary Experience. *Makustele.* 34-37.

Hull, J.S., Patterson, C., Huijbens, E. & S.S. Milne (2008a). *The State of Affairs of Tourism in Northeast Iceland. Report #1.* Húsavík, Iceland: Atthing.

Hull, J.S., Patterson, C., Huijbens, E. & S.S. Milne. (2008b). *The Tourism Strategic Plan for Northeast Iceland. 2009-2014. Report #2.* Húsavík, Iceland: Atthing.

Inn and Around (2009). *Lighthouses and Lighthouse Tours Around the Lower Great Lakes.* Retrieved April 15, 2009, from http://www.inn-and-a-round.com/lighthouses.htm

International Culinary Tourism Association (2009). *About Culinary Tourism*. Retrieved April 15, 2009, from http://www.culinarytourism.org/?page=intro

ITB (Icelandic Tourist Board) (2009). *Visit Iceland*. Retrieved February 20, 2009, from http://www.visiticeland.com/

ITB (Icelandic Tourist Board) (2005). *Tourism in Iceland in figures. 2005*. Reykjavik: Icelandic Tourism Board.

Kellogg. R. (2001). Introduction. In V. Hreinsson (Ed.) *The Complete Sagas of Icelanders*. (Vol. I) (pp. xxix-lv). Reykjavik, Iceland: Leifur Eiriksson Publishing.

Langanesbyggd (2009). *Northeast Iceland: Explore and Enjoy*. Retrieved April 15, 2009, from http://www.langanesbyggd.is/category.php?catID=17

McKercher, B. & H. du Cros. (2002). *Cultural Tourism: the partnership between tourism and cultural heritage management*. London: Haworth Press.

Moscardo, G. (2008). Community Capacity Buildling: an Emerging Challenge for Tourism Development. In G. Moscardo (Ed.) *Building Community Capacity for Tourism Development* (pp. 1-15). Wallingford, UK.: CABI International.

NORCE. (2009). *Northern Coastal Experience*. Retrieved February 15, 2009, from http://www.norce.org/

Norwegian Lighthouse Association (2009). *Lighthouse Vacations*. Retrieved April 15, 2009, from http://www.lighthouses.no/

Richards, G. (2001). The development of cultural tourism in Europe. In G. Richards (Ed.) Cultural Attractions and European Tourism (pp. 3-29). Wallingford, UK: CABI International.

Richards, G. (1996). The scope and significance of cultural tourism. In G. Richards (Ed.). *Cultural tourism in Europe* (pp. 19-46). Wallingford, UK: CABI International.

Smiley, J . (2001). Preface. In O. Thorsson (Ed.) *The Sagas of the Icelanders* (pp. ix-xiv). London, UK: Penguin Books.

Snow Magic (2009). *Snow Magic- English*. Retrieved April 15, 2009, from http://www.snowmagic.is/page.asp?Id=600

Statistics Iceland (2008). Tourism Satellite Accounts in Iceland 2000-2006. In Vilborg H. Júlíusdóttir & Jóhann Rúnar Björgvinsson (Eds.) *Statistical Series: Tourism and Transport* 93(59) (pp. 1-44). Reykjavík: Statistics Iceland.

Timothy, D. J. & S.W. Boyd (2003). *Heritage Tourism*. Essex, England: Prentice Hall.

UNESCO (2009). *1998 International year of the ocean: national contributions.* Retrieved February 25, 2009, from
http://ioc.unesco.org/iyo/activities/countries/iceland.htm

UNESCO (2009). *Definition of cultural heritage.* Retrieved April 15, 2009, from
http://portal.unesco.org/culture/en/ev.php-
URL_ID=34050&URL_DO=DO_TOPIC&URL_SECTION=201.html

UNWTO (2008). *UNWTO Tourism Highlights 2007.* Retrieved November 4, 2008, from http://www.unwto.org/facts/eng/highlights.htm

Viking Age Classics (1997). The Saga of Grettir the Strong. In V. Hreinsson (Ed.) *The Complete Sagas of Icelanders.* (Vol. II) (pp. 49-192). Reykjavik, Iceland: Leifur Eiriksson Publishing.

Zeppel, H. & C. M. Hall (1992). Arts and Heritage Tourism. In B. Weiler & C.M. Hall (Eds). *Special Interest Tourism.* (pp. 47-68). London: Belhaven.

Cultural Tourism in Germany:
A Look at different Perspectives

Anja Wollesen

1. Introduction

Although there is no standard definition of cultural tourism, there is, by now, a widespread distinction between two types of cultural tourists: The group of Special Cultural Tourists, who travel specifically because of the culture on offer, and the group of "Chance Cultural Tourists". For the latter, the cultural event is one option among many others available at their destination, but is not the main reason for their trip.

"The actual cultural tourism product is characterised by the cultural event being combined with other tourist services (....) and is amenable to the consumer by being effectively bookable".[1]

By the product development and marketing stage, at least two different viewpoints and perspectives stand out: The cultural dimension and the tourism dimension. For the former, cultural tourism is a mega trend, an image maker, an economic factor, for the latter, cultural tourism is the epitome of the "commodification" of culture. In this case marketing and the maximisation of profits are of equal importance.[2] The fear of selling off their cultural values is the reason for the diffidence of many cultural institutions when cooperation with tourism is called for.

At the same time, cultural tourism, seen spatially, has been long established as a market segment of tourism: The metropolises of Germany in particular have closely linked their City Tourism with Cultural Tourism. "Culture, in all its facets - from the cultural event to architecture - along with social aspects is by far the most important factor for tourists when choosing private city breaks".[3]

---

[1] Ostdeutscher Sparkassen- und Giroverband (2003): Tourismusbarometer – Jahresbericht 2003, Spezialthemen, p. 95.

[2] See also: Helm, S./Hausmann, A. (2006): Kundenorientierung im Kulturbetrieb, Grundlagen - innovative Konzepte - praktische Umsetzung, VS Verlag für Sozialwissenschaften, Wiesbaden, p. 16.

[3] DTV (Hrsg.)/dwif (2006): Städte- und Kulturtourismus in Deutschland, Langfassung, Bonn, p. 49.

Even rural regions are starting to focus more and more on the cultural tourism market segment. The culture on offer is pivotal to the development of unique selling propositions. As well as the natural surroundings, culture is what is unique and distinctive and that can only be found in this place or region. Culture helps to animate the special features of a region, to give it its unmistakable character. There are countless examples of successful cultural tourism cooperation and networking between culture and tourism to show that use can be made of different interests which benefit all parties.

In regional development processes, the aim today is to create so-called "creative clusters", a "convergence of competing, cooperating or independent companies and institutions which are connected by a system of economic or non-profit tie-ins and in many cases are also regionally connected".[4] Cultural establishments can in this way, from the independent operational point of view, be put into a larger (economic) context.[5]

What follows is the attempt to illustrate different perspectives of culture tourism in Germany: From the presentation of the facts to the viewpoints; from the ideas and visions to their implementation.

---

[4] Erster Österreichische Kreativwirtschaftsbericht (EÖKW) in Klein, A. (2007): Der exzellente Kulturbetrieb, VS Verlag für Sozialwissenschaften, Wiesbaden, p. 264.
[5] Cf. Ibid. p. 265.

2. Facts and Figures

2.1 Cultural tourism attractions and activities

Germany is rich in cultural treasures: 5000 museums (500 of which are art galleries), 300 theatres, over 100 musical theatres und opera houses, 130 professional orchestras, 7500 libraries are all evidence of the variety of culture on offer, available in a density which is hardly to be found in another country. "German writers, composers and philosophers such as Goethe, Schiller, Bach, Beethoven, Kant and Hegel shaped cultural epochs and still enjoy a significant status today".[6]

2000 years of European cultural history have left their mark on Germany. It is hard to find another country in which there is such a concentration of unique natural and cultural monuments. 34 of these are designated as having "extraordinary universal value" for mankind, and have been placed under protection by UNESCO. These include among others, individual buildings, ensembles of cities, palaces and gardens as well as 180 thematic cultural and historical routes.

2.2 Demand for cultural tourism

Cultural tourism is no longer only considered a mega trend and growth market by tourism professionals. The market share of the "pure" cultural tourists, who travel because of culture, accounts for only 4 per cent of the German travel market. However, even though culture is not the determining factor for the majority of travellers, there are a lot of "chance cultural tourists": 80 million tourists avail of cultural attractions and activities during day trips, short trips and holidays.[7] A total of € 82 billion gross turnover is earned in city and cultural tourism every year in Germany.[8]

---

[6] http://www.tatsachen-ueber-deutschland.de/de/inhaltsseiten-home/zahlen-fakten/kultur, 21.07.2009.

[7] MWFK Brandenburg / TMB (2005): Leitfaden Kulturtourismus in Brandenburg, Potsdam, p. 6.

[8] Deutscher Tourismusverband (DTV) (publ.) dwif (2006), Städte- und Kultur-tourismus, abridged version, p. 10.

For cultural tourists in the broader sense, culture is a commensurate part of the holiday along with other possible leisure activities. According to Opaschowski, a leisure expert, the travel market is one of the few areas which will show significant growth in the future.[9] 77 per cent of all German travellers at least occasionally visit cultural sights such as museums while on holiday.[10]

This trend is corroborated by foreign travellers: In 2005 a survey was carried out in various European countries on behalf of the German Centre for Tourism, to ascertain what image Germany has as a travel destination. Every second respondent stated that Germany offers a great deal for a cultural holiday and has attractive city break destinations. Almost two thirds were of the opinion that that Germany has attractive sights. Sightseeing (55%), visiting museums (36%) and exhibitions (25%) are among the main activities undertaken by Europeans during city breaks and tours in Germany.[11]

"Germany is the second most popular destination for European cultural tourists. Germany is only second to France with a share of 10 per cent of all cultural trips taken by Europeans. For the first time, more culture and art enthusiasts travelled to Germany than to Italy. According to World Travel Monitor (WTM), the number of European cultural tourists to Germany has risen by about 30 per cent since the year 2000. Among the most popular activities are visits to museums and exhibitions."[12]

The demand for cultural tourism is particularly evident in the metropolises, as the example of the capital, Berlin, clearly shows: According to information from "Qualitätsmonitor Deutschlandtourismus", 71 per cent of guests to Berlin in 2008 came because of the art and culture on offer in the capital. A recent survey was carried out at the end of 2008 by "Kulmon", a visitor research project initiated by the Berlin Culture Department and the Berlin Tourism Marketing GmbH (BTM) in cooperation with seven major Berlin cultural establishments. In the press releases about the results of the first lot of polls, it is said:

---

[9] B.A.T. Freizeitforschungsinstitut (2007), in: Nordfriesland Tageblatt, 5.3.2007.

[10] MWFK Brandenburg / TMB (2005): Leitfaden Kulturtourismus in Brandenburg, Potsdam, p. 6.

[11] Cf. DTV (publ.)/dwif (2006), Städte- und Kulturtourismus, unabridged version, p. 60.

[12] Cf. Die Bundesregierung, e.conomy das wirtschaftsmagazin, Nr. 048 07/2007, p. 6.

"Culture is a major incentive to travel. In answer to the question whether a visit to a museum or an arts performance was the main reason for travelling to Berlin, 61.3 percent of the non-resident theatre goers and 43.38 percent of the non-resident museum visitors responded affirmatively. Visitors to Berlin who are culturally active, stayed longer: The average length of stay of museum visitors was 4.39 days according to a survey and 3.67 days for theatre goers. In comparison: The average length of stay of all visitors to Berlin who stayed in paid accommodation was 2.2 days in 2008".[13]

According to a survey on marketing strategies in approx 250 cultural establishments in 19 European cities, museums, on the whole, make a greater contribution to tourism than other cultural establishments. The survey ascertained that tourists accounted for an average of 39 per cent of all visitors to 120 museums in European cities. The identified share of the total number of visitors to other cultural establishments (such as concert venues, theatres, operettas and musicals) was approx. 12 per cent.[14]

3. Role perception

3.1 The role of culture in tourism

From a tourism perspective, cultural activities are first and foremost part of the general and specific infrastructure of a tourist destination. Cultural establishments complement the leisure and adventure activities of a region. The combination of the cultural experience with the basic tourist package of accommodation and catering comprises an "overall cultural tourism package", which ideally can also be booked as such.

What makes the cultural activity special, is that it belongs to the "natural activities" of a region: hard to copy, unique and therefore creates a strong sense of identity. There is an opportunity for tourism marketing in the development of unique selling propositions: Every region has its very own culture which is apparent in different areas.

---

[13] http://www.destinet.de, 18.06.2009.
[14] Cf. Dümcke, C. (2002): „Kultur und Tourismus in den neuen Ländern – eine Untersuchung am Beispiel der kulturellen Leuchttürme und Gedächtnisorte", Studie im Auftrag des Beauftragten der Bundesregierung für Angelegenheiten der Kultur und der Medien (BKM), Berlin, p. 37/38.

"The cultural environment of a region is not only evident in its historical assets (churches, castles, farm houses, harbours, customs, language etc.), but also in the creative potential of contemporary theatre, concerts, musical events, museum and gallery exhibitions, readings etc."[15]

"For tourism, culturally related activities play a special role as so-called tourist 'frequency generators' or 'frequency boosting activities'."[16] "A state comparison relating to marketing at federal state level shows that culture tourism themes have had a special significance in the tourism marketing of the German federal states since the mid-90s."[17]

The range of activities is wide: from literature and music performances in Baden-Württemburg to the bid for the World Cultural Heritage sites in Saxony-Anhalt and Brandenburg to architecture of museum quality in Nordrhein-Westphalia... Even a look at the websites of the individual state marketing organisations offers a seemingly endless range of cultural attractions and specialties in each federal state. Given the wealth of cultural activities it is understandable that culture constitutes an umbrella brand in tourism marketing for many federal states.

The potential benefits for the destination as a result of the development of culture tourism are multilayer and are summarized as follows:[18]

- Culture tourism activities (...), have an overall positive effect on the municipalities.
- The tourist industry (...) profits directly from additional visitors.
- The local economy benefits from the culture tourists, because they spend about three to four times the amount other tourists spend.
- This in turn secures jobs and creates new jobs.

---

[15] Heinze, T. (1999): „Kulturtourismus. Grundlagen, Trends und Fallstudien", Oldenbourg Verlag, München, p. 8.

[16] Arbeitsgemeinschaft Kulturwirtschaft LSA 2001, p. 98.

[17] Dümcke, C. (2002): „Kultur und Tourismus in den neuen Ländern – eine Untersuchung am Beispiel der kulturellen Leuchttürme und Gedächtnisorte", Studie im Auftrag des Beauftragten der Bundesregierung für Angelegenheiten der Kultur und der Medien (BKM), Berlin, p. 15.

[18] Klein, A. (2007): „Der exzellente Kulturbetrieb", VS Verlag für Sozialwissenschaften, Wiesbaden, p. 284.

- The image of a city and city marketing benefit from interesting cultural activities (...)
- This can be an important criteria for new companies setting up in a location: A company would much rather set up in an a municipality with a strong cultural image and a corresponding vibrancy than in one with a bad public image, providing, of course, that the other factors are conducive.

Many federal states are working on a long term strategy to develop sustainable culture tourism. North Rhine-Westphalia, for example, has set up consultancies to develop culture in the region. Their website states:[19]

"The aim of our regional cultural policy is to cultivate regional identity with instruments of art and culture. At the same time we wish to contribute to an improved network of cultural establishments within the state and to encourage local artists to work together. Regional cultural support programmes are instrumental in this. Projects from all the arts are considered, including projects with children and youths and intercultural projects. Many of the projects are of great interest to culture-tourists (.....)."

In its state cultural report, Saxony-Anhalt presented a comprehensive analysis of the requirements for the development of culture tourism in each of the regions. Among other things it states:

"The varying development and the very distinctive target groups of the tourist region are not due to the different marketing strategies of the various tourist institutions, but mainly as a result of the special activities in each region."

The cultural report presents the analysed potential of each region as well as development indicators.[20]

---

[19] http//:www.kultur.nrw.de/regionale_kulturpolitik/index.html, 26.07.2009.
[20] LSA (2001/02): 1. Kulturwirtschaftsbericht Sachsen-Anhalt. Hauptteil und Zusammenfassung. Magdeburg/Bonn.

3.2 The role of tourism in culture

While the tourism industry is almost exclusively determined by the market and therefore depends on demand, the priority of the public cultural establishments is to fulfil its cultural and educational mandate.

"The interest of the establishments in attracting more and more visitors is a point of conflict for most of the establishments (…) There appears to be a conflict between the function of the establishments to protect the cultural assets and the economic pressure to increase the number of visitors."[21]

Depending on the cultural sector, specific tasks are stipulated which have to be carried out by the cultural establishments. The work of the museums is described by the International Council of Museums (ICOM) as follows:

"a non-profit making, permanent institution in the service of society and of its development, and open to the public, which acquires, conserves, researches, communicates and exhibits, for purposes of study, education and enjoyment, material evidence of people and their environment"[22]

The main tasks assigned to the museums "acquisition, conservation, research und exhibiting/communicating" are the basis for the work of a museum. Today, however, the museum federation has a more extended focal point regarding the tasks of exhibiting and communicating.

Visitor orientation constitutes an important part of museum work, but it is emphasised that the protection of cultural assets is a priority. The German Museum Federation writes on its website:

"Both opportunities and problems alike, provide tourist museums with a culture consisting of events and fun and the dwindling differentiation between e-culture and u-culture : While museums are now recognised as a strong location factor in tourism today, and many more people are visiting museums thanks to additional activities, droves of visitors or "events" pose threats to the conservation of the artefacts or degrade them to mere accessories."[23]

---

[21] Cf. Dümcke, C. (2002): „Kultur und Tourismus in den neuen Ländern – eine Untersuchung am Beispiel der kulturellen Leuchttürme und Gedächtnisorte", Studie im Auftrag des Beauftragten der Bundesregierung für Angelegenheiten der Kultur und der Medien (BKM), Berlin, p. 41.

[22] http://icom.museum/hist_def_eng.html.

[23] http://www.museumsbund.de/index., 26.07.2009.

"This conflict of interest can be ascribed to the special characteristics of cultural assets and services as unique assets, which have to do with identity, ideals and appreciation and cannot be seen as goods or consumer durables."[24]

Reason enough for many cultural establishments to be reserved about cooperating with tourism. The fear of being "over-marketed" is still strong. Marketing is often misinterpreted in terms of its aims and content.

"Marketing is basically about managing competitive advantages. (...) Competition in the cultural sector includes not only the procurement of visitors, but also acquiring financial support from public authorities, getting qualified staff etc. and recruiting cooperation partners."[25]

Klein (2007) explains quite clearly, that visitor orientation is compatible with the cultural brief of institutions, when he says:

"Consistent visitor orientation does not mean just offering what the public wants, as is often maliciously insinuated. What it in fact means, is that the cultural institutions undertake every endeavour to communicate the artistic-aesthetic product to as many people as possible."[26]

It can be concluded that

"museums today are faced with the task of combining traditional tasks with new functions, the functions of research and education as well as a service orientation, which is rewarding for the visitor and sustainable for the museum itself."[27]

---

[24] Dümcke, C. (2002): „Kultur und Tourismus in den neuen Ländern – eine Untersuchung am Beispiel der kulturellen Leuchttürme und Gedächtnisorte", Studie im Auftrag des Beauftragten der Bundesregierung für Angelegenheiten der Kultur und der Medien (BKM), Berlin, p. 75.

[25] Cf. Helm, S. / Hausmann, A. (2006): „Kundenorientierung im Kulturbetrieb, Grundlagen - innovative Konzepte - praktische Umsetzung", VS Verlag für Sozialwissenschaften, Wiesbaden, p. 17.

[26] Klein, A. (2007): „Der exzellente Kulturbetrieb", VS Verlag für Sozialwissen- schaften, Wiesbaden, p. 100.

[27] Koch, A. (2002): „Museumsmarketing: Ziele, Strategien, Maßnahmen. Mit einer Analyse der Hamburger Kunsthalle". In: Schriften zum Kultur- und Museumsmanagement, Transcript Verlag, Bielefeld, p. 56.

The prerequisites for the successful development and implementation of cultural tourism is a coordinated process, mutually supported by both culture and tourism. Only in this way can sustainable cooperation be established between regional and local policy makers and experts from culture and tourism.

The beginning of such a development may sound banal, but it has proved its worth. It all starts with communication: Listening, communicating, learning about the functions and structures of the other areas etc. ... The basis for joint development and marketing of culture tourism products.

This is confirmed by the results of a culture tourism study of the west coast of Schleswig-Holstein carried out by the Institute for Management and Tourism (IMT) from 2005-2007. The aim of the project was to establish the collective opportunities of culture and tourism in the regions of Nordfriesland and Dithmarschen and to identify the potential for development. The detailed results can be found in "Leitfaden für Regionen zur Entwicklung kulturtouristischer Produkte (Guidelines for the regional development of culture tourism products)"[28]. What follows is a summary of the fields of activity which were identified and developed in this project.

4. Success factors in the development of culture tourism as exemplified by the West Coast of Schleswig-Holstein, IMT Project (2005-2007)

Culture and tourism can - and should - be mutually beneficial. By developing cultural focal points, tourist destinations can improve the image of their region and thus improve their competitiveness. Cultural establishments have the chance to increase their economic viability by not only fulfilling the traditional function of museum work, but also meeting the demands of the tourist market.

Making use of synergies for culture and tourism, developing strengths and minimising weaknesses were the starting points for the research

---

[28] Cf. Eisenstein, B. / Maschewski, A. (2007): Leitfaden zur Entwicklung kulturtouristischer Produkte am Beispiel der Kreise Nordfriesland und Dithmarschen, Institut für Management und Tourismus der Fachhochschule Westküste, Heide.

project "Culture and tourism in the regions of Nordfriesland and Dithmarschen". The main aim of the project was to find ways to make cooperation between culture and tourism attractive in rural regions. This is quite a challenge given the clustered structure which characterises these destinations. Unlike in large tourist centres, cultural potential is not immediately evident in rural regions: Inadequate cooperation structures, few marketable products, a lack of marketing and communication concepts, little coordination with the existing tourist structures are just some of the reasons why action needs to be taken. It is not only necessary in the North Sea regions of Schleswig-Holstein, the same is true for many other regions in the various federal states.

The aim of the project "Culture and Tourism in the regions of Nordfriesland and Dithmarschen" was, therefore, to offer concrete starting points for local cultural tourist cooperation beyond the strategic level of cultural tourism, which ideally can benefit other regions, too. The framework is formed by four fields of operation which should be at the very fore in the development of culture and tourism in both regions in the future:

Product development
- The development of new target group oriented and market-driven cultural tourist attractions and activities.
- Improving existing products.
- Increased correlation and differentiation of themes.
- Consideration of the clustered structure of the regions of Nordfriesland and Dithmarschen.

Culture Tourism Qualifications
- Collecting training proposals for tourism organisations and cultural establishments.
- Consulting cultural establishments and culture tourism protagonists.
- Training tour guides.

Communication
- Increasing the visibility of attractions and activities.
- Target group-oriented processing of information relevant to culture tourism activities.

- Development of suitable information and communication platforms for people playing an active role in tourism at local and regional level.
- Linking up with the cultural platform of the state of Schleswig-Holstein.
- Development of a "product development platform" for people involved in culture and tourism.

Cooperation and Organisation

- Continuation and development of cooperation between cultural and tourism institutions and third parties.
- Pooling culture tourism marketing activities for the whole North Sea destination via NTS.
- Increasing cooperation between culture and business.
- Setting up a new central body for culture and tourism in both regions of Nordfriesland and Dithmarschen:
  (1) to develop and improve the potential for culture tourism,
  (2) as a continuous impetus for new activities,
  (3) for product development tailored to the target market,
  (4) for coordination and cooperation,
  (5) as well as for quality assurance.

4.1 Success Factor: Product development

Like any other tourist, the cultural tourist wants a tourist package - rather than the individual cultural attractions and activities. The function of the regional partner is to create an attractive package consisting of several tourist components: cultural attractions, natural settings, catering, transport services, accommodation, events etc. Ideally, it should be possible to combine various elements at will.

Once the potential of the regional cultural attractions has been discovered for tourism, it has to be decided how they it can be put to use. When the variety of the regional attractions and activities have been bundled, sorted according to themes and communicated and marketed to specific target groups, then and only then can it be "used" for tourism. In tourism terminology, this is known as "tourism application". "Each basic offer, each natural/cultural space, resource and potential must first be valued/rated. That means it has to be assigned a value in order for it to be marketable. (...)

A culture tourism application always encompasses the provision of infrastructures (from "performance structures") to the hotel and restaurant industry to information material and public thoroughfares."[29]

In the tourist destination, two crucial questions must be answered at the beginning of product development:

- Which capable parties involved in culture and tourism are available in the region who can work together to create attractive culture tourism products?
- Who are the visitors who have been travelling to the region and what are their demands and motivation?

On the west coast of Schleswig-Holstein two target groups have long been centre stage in the marketing of the Nordsee Tourismus Service (NTS): families with children and the 50+ age group. They have been the strongest market for the North Sea destinations of Schleswig-Holstein for years now and have been used and developed accordingly for culture tourism.[30] To guarantee the quality of the existing attractions in the region, the activities and attractions available were evaluated according to target groups and were analysed in four steps:

- SWOT analysis regarding the quality of the attractions, the communication structures, the cooperation and organisation of culture and tourism in both regions.
- Target group oriented mystery check of 43 cultural establishments as regards features, organisation and marketing
- Target group specific description and evaluation of the packages available.
- Analysis of the regional culture tourism guided tours.

---

[29] Ibid. Heinze, T. (1997): Kulturtourismus: Grundlagen, Trends und Fallstudien, Oldenbourg Verlag, München.

[30] Cf. N.I.T. (2004): Evaluation des Tourismuskonzeptes Nordfriesland, Kiel.

4.2 Success factor: Communication

One of the main causes of the limited communication between culture and tourism to date, is clearly a lack of information in the culture tourism establishments and among stakeholders. Most of the service providers simply do not have the time to embark on time consuming research. The large scale dispersal of the cultural attractions and activities requires the project management to have a high degree of coordination.

Many of the small cultural establishments do not have either the staff or the financial means to take on additional tasks such as product development and marketing. The consequences are that if there is no coordination, the cultural activities and attractions remain in obscurity.

All the data on culture and tourism collected during this project has been processed in comprehensive excel files and made available to interested parties. This includes lists of:

- Cultural establishments (inventory and checklists),
- artists on the west coast,
- historical buildings, "beauty spots",
- culture tourism packages,
- tour guides,
- cycling trips, themed routes,
- pool of ideas for literary events (products + organisation),
- pool of ideas for children/family products (+ organisation),
- overview of all tourism organisations on the west coast.

4.3 Success factor: organisation structure

Successful implementation ultimately depends on well functioning organisational structures, this is also true of cultural tourism. The numerous creative and promising ideas which developed in the course of the project with parties from culture and tourism can only be implemented if the responsibility remains with professionals, even once the project is over.

The development of products for cultural tourism requires a great deal of coordination especially in rural areas. This can not be achieved unless it is clear who is responsible.

4.4   Success factor: qualified staff

The tasks involved in the development and marketing of products for cultural tourism are multilayer and require special skills: Ranging from knowledge of the regional and nationwide tourism industry and the cultural scene to experience with grant application processes, to tourism marketing and event planning. The finished project demonstrated, if nothing else, how multilayered the scope of duties is for the development of culture and tourism in the regions of Nordfriesland and Dithmarschen. Only few service providers can offer this spectrum – expertise must be bought in as deemed necessary.

It is precisely at this point that the endeavours of the joint development of culture and tourism fail. The existing staff cannot cope with the additional tasks- particularly as both areas are usually poorly staffed.

If culture and tourism are to continue to grow together and to be of long-term mutual benefit, additional financial and personnel resources are absolutely essential. It seems to be necessary at this point to provide support, including structural support, beyond the mere financial support of cultural and tourism organizations.

References

B.A.T. Freizeitforschungsinstitut (2007), zitiert in: Nordfriesland Tageblatt vom 5.3.2007.

DTV (Hrsg.)/dwif (2006): *Städte- und Kulturtourismus in Deutschland*, Langfassung, Bonn.

Dümcke, C. (2002): *Kultur und Tourismus in den neuen Ländern – eine Untersuchung am Beispiel der kulturellen Leuchttürme und Gedächtnisorte*, Studie im Auftrag des Beauftragten der Bundesregierung für Angelegenheiten der Kultur und der Medien (BKM), Berlin.

Eisenstein, B./Maschewski, A. (2007): *Leitfaden zur Entwicklung kulturtouristischer Produkte am Beispiel der Kreise Nordfriesland und Dithmarschen*, Institut für Management und Tourismus der Fachhochschule Westküste, Heide.

Heinze, T. (1999): Kulturtourismus: Grundlagen, Trends und Fallstudien, Oldenbourg Verlag, München.

Helm, S./Hausmann, A. (2006): Kundenorientierung im Kulturbetrieb, Grundlagen - innovative Konzepte - praktische Umsetzung, VS Verlag für Sozialwissenschaften, Wiesbaden.

Klein, A. (2007): Der exzellente Kulturbetrieb, VS Verlag für Sozialwissenschaften, Wiesbaden.

Koch, A. (2002): *Museumsmarketing: Ziele, Strategien, Maßnahmen. Mit einer Analyse der Hamburger Kunsthalle.* In: Schriften zum Kultur- und Museumsmanagement, Transcript Verlag, Bielefeld.

Land Sachsen-Anhalt (2001/02): *Erster Kulturwirtschaftsbericht Sachsen-Anhalt. Hauptteil und Zusammenfassung.* Magdeburg/Bonn.

Ministerium für Wissenschaft, Forschung und Kultur des Landes Brandenburg / TMB Tourismus-Marketing-Brandenburg GmbH (publ.) (2005): *Leitfaden Kulturtourismus in Brandenburg*, Potsdam.

N.I.T. (2004): *Evaluation des Tourismuskonzeptes Nordfriesland*, Kiel.

Ostdeutscher Sparkassen- und Giroverband (2003): *Tourismusbarometer – Jahresbericht 2003, Spezialthemen*, Berlin.

The Influence of Culture on Student Travel Behaviour

Elmarie Slabbert, Peet van der Merwe

1. Introduction

Travel behaviour is the result of an attempt to satisfy unfulfilled needs, such as relaxation and spending time with family and friends (Nylen, as cited by Kotze, 2005). It refers to what people do over a specific time and is influenced by various factors including personality, lifestyles, tourist-roles and culture (Pizam & Sussmann, 1995). Carr (2002) stated that behaviour is also influenced by a combination of socio-cultural norms, values and personal motivations that are present in both the home and holiday environments. This implies that travel behaviour, motives and destination choices differ according to the life cycle of the tourist (Opperman, 1995), previous experiences, personal barriers and age, to name a few.

There has been a considerable research interest in travel behaviour and, according to Pizam and Sussmann (1995), various studies have indicated the influence of nationality and race on travel behaviour (Zmud & Arca, 1998). The literature review, however, indicates that the latter has not been researched in depth and therefore studies seeking to account for differences in tourist behaviour are justified.

The student travel market has shown significant growth over the past few years, especially in South Africa and, according to Schrage, Shoham and Van Eeden (2001), college-age students travel more than generations before them did. Travel is easier than it ever has been and this leads to new and extended opportunities for students to travel (Shoham, Schrage & Van Eeden, 2004). It is thus important to analyse the travel behaviour of this growing market to fulfil their needs with the right products and marketing practices. Therefore the aim of this article is to compare the travel behaviour of tourism students from selected universities in South Africa based on race.

This article is organised as follows: the literature review and problem statement follows the introduction, after which the method of research and results will be discussed. Lastly, implications are analysed followed by conclusions and recommendations.

2. Literature Review

Tourism can be considered as an experience which is produced and consumed at the same time (Heung, Qu & Chu, 2001). Travelling has become popular for many reasons including an increase in leisure time and income, improvements in technological processes which speed up the process of bookings, the transfer of money, and travelling in general (Yau & Chan, 1990; Hsu & Sung, 1997, Shoham et al., 2004). With this in mind, it is important to understand motivations for travel as well as the factors that influence destination choices as such understanding can assist in tourism product planning and marketing. Younger tourists, such as students, are spending more time on travel planning, especially on aspects such as the destination, the mode of travel, and the cost of the trip (Goodhall & Ashworth, 1998).

Hsu and Sung (1997), as well as Carr (2005), indicated that students have become an important segment of the tourism industry due to long holiday breaks, increased mobility, independence, and the fact that they live far from their parents, which leaves them with enough time to travel. It has become easier for students to travel and explore their own country as well as the world. Travelling abroad provides a richer tourism experience as well as a mutual intercultural understanding. Gallarza and Saura (2006) highlighted that students are a relatively unattended segment that has attracted the attention of many researchers due to the growth in the number of students engaging in holiday breaks and the consumption of very particular tourism services. Therefore it is important to understand the travel behaviour of this growing segment as this is the traveller of tomorrow.

Although young adults tend to be constrained by relatively low levels of disposable income, the fact that they have few commitments such as children and dependant spouses as well as ample free time allows them a high level of propensity. Awareness of their travel needs and preferences is therefore important. The travel behaviour of students is further encouraged by society's view of student lifestyles, peer pressure to conform to the travel-orientated image of students and parental expectations of students' travel behaviour (Carr, 2005).

Younger travellers, such as students, belong to a number of different sub-cultures at any one time that are related to age, gender, race and a variety of other personal characteristics (Carr, 2002). The latter found that tourists' culture and cultural baggage may not be discrete entities and that both may influence travel behaviour. Tourists' culture may therefore be partially determined by the society and partially by their home culture. Even though Figure 1 identifies culture and personal motivations as separate influences on tourism behaviour, it is an oversimplification to say there is no relation between them. Rather, motivation and socio-cultural norms and values are more accurately viewed as interrelated entities that are constantly changing as a result of people's interaction with one another. It is also important to note how the behaviour of people may be influenced by personal characteristics such as age and gender.

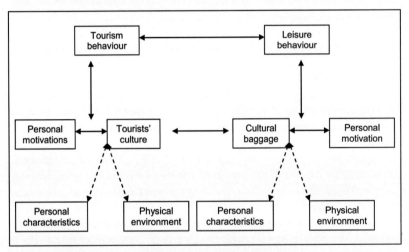

Fig. 1: A model of the tourism-leisure continuum[1]

Various factors can therefore influence travel behaviour. Heung et al., (2001) identified six factors influencing the travel decision-making process. These include the perceptions of the individual, previous experiences, motivation to visit the destination, information search, and attitudes as well as intentions. Dellaert, Ettema and Lindh (1998) added traveller characteristics such as number of people in the travel group, traveller income, age, and possible relationships with people at certain destinations. In 2001 Hsu and Kang (2001), as well as Saayman (2001),

---

[1] Adapted from Carr, 2002.

added length of trip, characteristics of a particular destination, travel budget, activities to participate in, accommodation, type of travel, method of travel and the influence of tour organisations and services. A more recent study by McKercher, Wong and Lau (2006), found that time is one of the few absolutes that tourists must face, for time cannot be stored for use in the future. Decisions regarding the effective use of time are related to both the absolute amount of time available and also to the set of activities the tourist wishes to consume during his or her stay.

The factors indicated by Heung et al., (2001) can be seen as the factors influencing the choice sets of the tourists and factors indicated by Saayman (2001) and Hsu and Kang (2001), can be seen as the choice sets of the tourists.

Choice sets tourists (students) have to decide on before travelling:

(1) Method of travel
The type of transport will depend on the type of person as well as the reason for travelling. The cost of transport is part of the travel budget and directly influences the choice of tourism destination (Kotze, 2005). Böhler, Grischat and Hunecke (2005) support this by stating that transport decisions are also dependent on the choice of destination. Travelling by car is still the preferred choice of transport for students in South Africa since the public transport system is perceived as unsafe. However, many students do not have the financial resources to afford a car and this can inhibit travel. Travelling by bus is popular and more affordable, and it is also considered as a fairly safe way to travel. Poor infrastructure and high costs make travelling by train and airplane less popular (Michael, Armstrong & King, 2003). In the USA, similar results have been obtained indicating that most students travel by car, followed by airplane, bus and train. Given the distance between the destination and the university, as well as the amount of time available, it was not surprising that many students flew to their destinations. However, the majority of trips were by car (Hobson & Josiam, 1992). International students and backpackers tend to travel by bus, although renting cars was also popular. Research by Pearce and Son (2004) indicated that travelling by train was more popular with international students. It is therefore clear that preferences differ in terms of transport.

(2) Accommodation
Accommodation refers to hotels, guesthouses, backpacker units, camping sites and so on. In South Africa there is a growing need for more accommodation due to the increase in the number of tourists (Saayman, 2000). South African students prefer to stay with friends and family when travelling. In many cases family and friends are spread throughout the country and staying with them is seen as an opportunity to save money (Michael et al., 2003). On the international front, however, preferences differ. Hotels and motels are the most popular form of accommodation for international students, while backpackers are less likely to use hotels or motels (Pearce & Son, 2004). It seems that price plays an important role when considering accommodation options. Different types of accommodation should be provided for tourists while travelling.

(3) Destination
Destinations are viewed differently by different types of tourists. A tourist's destination choice is influenced by a variety of personal and environmental factors (Kotze, 2005). According to Saayman (2001), non-destination related motivations are easier to determine than those that are destination related. Motivators that are non-destination related give the tourist little to no choice of visiting that destination. These non-destination related reasons are business journeys and travelling for health reasons. Destination related motives are those motives that give tourists the opportunity to choose the destination they want to visit. Tourists can thus compare destinations and then decide which destination is most attractive to them. Students may be influenced by aspects such as activities at the destination, opportunities for socialising and cost.

(4) Time and duration of stay
The growth of leisure time in the past century brought about by technological and other improvements has greatly increased the amount of time available for travel. Most students plan the trip/vacation four to six months in advance (McKercher et al., 2006). In Australia, students prefer to travel during the summer break (December-February), followed by the semester break in July between semesters 1 and 2 (the southern winter) (Michael et al., 2003). The same pattern is followed in South Africa as various students also take a vacation during the summer

(December-February) and winter (June-July). This is directly related to school holidays or summer/winter breaks at the universities.

(5) Travel size and group
Pearce and Son (2004) found that the international students were likely to travel in groups. This study showed that students travelled with one or more companions but also that some travelled alone.

However, these choice sets do not stand alone, but are influenced by certain factors such as income, motivation and culture. These factors will be discussed next.

(6) Perceptions of the individual
Perception can be defined as the process used by individuals to receive, select, organise and interpret information to create a meaningful image of the world (Kotze, 2005). According to Um and Crompton (1990), an individual's perception of a destination can be influenced by internal and external input. Therefore media, word-of-mouth, and past experiences play a role in decision making and travel behaviour. Harvey (2005) found that the youth are becoming more and more interested in the cultural aspects of a destination as well as the local music and sport.

(7) Income and budget
According to Harvey (2005), youth travellers spend exactly the same amount of money as older travellers. The difference is that they spend it over an extended period and not three days. Students tend to cut on accommodation to afford recreation activities. Tourists are more likely to have an approximate budget, but allow themselves flexibility in terms of spending. When it comes to actual trip spending, tourists are more likely to spend the same amount of money as expected or even less. Only one out of five tourists spends more than anticipated when travelling. Tourists who save money on transport to a destination are likely to spend more on other travel components, such as accommodation or activities (Patkose, Stokes & Cook, 2005).

Younger people who are single, and older people in the empty nest stage, have relatively more discretionary income and time than those in other stages. Income is higher as younger people do not have mortgage payments or children to support and they have more free time.

(8) Motivation of the individual

Realisation of unsatisfied needs drives tourists to travel. This drive is the motivation that triggers the tourist's travel decision-making process. Tourists are motivated by various aspects such as the need to relax, to spend time with family and friends, to learn about other cultures or to enjoy the scenic beauty of a specific destination. The motivation urges tourists to obtain information from family and friends, information offices and media to make travel decisions (Kotze, 2005). The importance of word-of-mouth is underestimated most of the time and students are directly influenced by friends and family in terms of travel choices.

(9) Culture

In recent years there has been considerable interest in the cultural aspect of tourism (Reisinger & Turner, 2003). Culture in its various forms and dimensions has a significant impact on tourism planning, development, management and marketing (Taylor, 2006). Tourism has experienced a growing internationalisation, and more attention is being paid to cultural diversity and its influence on travel behaviour and patterns.

(10) Marketing

Heung et al., (2001) suggest that different promotional strategies should be addressed to different segments of tourists with different travel motives. Sources of information can be categorised internally or externally. Internal sources of information relate to previous experiences, whereas external sources refer to information provided by travel agencies, friends and family, magazines and other travel organisations.

It is clear from the discussion above that differences may exist concerning the travel behaviour of students. From this perspective, various studies have been conducted concerning student travel. These studies focused on different types of students and countries and therefore the findings differed. Students from Australia do not favour packaged tours and they use internal sources for travel information. They tend to travel on holidays between one and seven days and rely mainly on their own savings for travel (Carr, 2003). A study done in Australia by Michael, Armstrong and King (2003) focused on motivations for travel and found that recommendations by friends and family, good beaches, the variety of attractions and scenic beauty motivated them to travel.

Hsu and Sung (quoted by Michael et al., 2003) found that some of the respondents preferred to make their own travel arrangements, while others made use of tour packages. Furthermore, they found that international students prefer to travel with cars, stay in hotels/motels and eat at fast-food restaurants while travelling. Western Australia studies show that overseas students travel by private road and public transport (much more than tourists in general) and also rented cars while travelling.

In 2003, Michael et al. (2003) found that students spent an average of $392.00 per trip (the biggest part on accommodation and transport) and they take approximately 1.8 to 2.3 trips per year. Hobson and Josiam (1992) stated that spring break is the most popular time for students to travel in America.

It is therefore clear that students' travel behaviour differs and that no consistent pattern could be identified between the various studies. This highlights the importance of this study which has not been conducted in South Africa. It is important to understand travel behaviour and factors influencing travel behaviour as this could assist in tourism planning and marketing. Table 1 highlights previous research on travel behaviour and, more specifically, the findings thereof.

Author/s	Main findings	Aim of research
Carr (2005)	• Engage in vacation at least once a year for 16.7 days • Paid for these vacations using a combination of personal savings and money from parents • Enjoy sightseeing • Make use of budget accommodation such as hostels as well as friends and relatives • Conduct own travel arrangements instead of making use of travel agents	Aim: to access the nature of the holiday experience of the university students population in England and Wales within the context of their financial position
Tal and Handy (2005)	• Found that white citizens made more use of own transport where black citizens make more use of community transport for travel proposes	Examine the relationship between travel behaviour and immigrant status
Zmud and Arce (1998)	• Found that culture influences travel behaviour trip purpose of long distance travel • Consumer travel of African Americans and Hispanics is much more family and group orientated that white travel • African Americans and Hispanics are more likely to make use of public transport that white travellers	Examine the intersection of consumer culture and travel behaviour
Pizam and Sussmann (1995)	• The results showed that Japanese keep mostly to themselves • American tourists tend to socialise more • Americans and Italians were more interested in people than artefacts • Japanese, French and Italian tourists avoid local foods, whereas Americans had a slight preference for local foods • Americans tend to take longer trips • Italian and French tourists were more adventurous • Japanese tourists tend to travel in groups while French tourists travel alone	To identify the perceptions that British tour guides had of four nationalities and to test whether there were significant differences by nationality in these perceptions

Tab. 1: Previous research regarding travel behaviour

Hence this research aims to compare the travel patterns of tourism students in South Africa based on race.

3.   Research Method

To be able to achieve the aim of this article, six tertiary training institutions offering Tourism as either a degree or a diploma were used to collate the information including Nelson Mandela Metropolitan University (Eastern Cape), University of Pretoria (Gauteng), Walter Sisulu University (Eastern Cape), Tshwane University of Technology (Gauteng), Central University of Technology (Free State) and North West University (North West). Data were collected by means of a structured questionnaire from second and third year students enrolled at the respective universities for tourism studies during 2006. The questionnaire was developed consisting of open and closed questions, as well as questions based on a 4-point Likert scale. Section A of the questionnaire focused on the demographic profile, Section B sought to determine the travel preferences and behaviour, and Section C focused on factors influencing travel choices. For the purpose of this article, the travel behaviour and factors influencing travel choices as well as race were used for the data analysis.

Tertiary institutions offering tourism as a subject were contacted and requested to take part in the study. Depending on the number of students, either third year students or second year students or third and second year students were included in the study. The questionnaire was completed by the number of students attending a specific contact session and was therefore based on availability sampling. This resulted in 610 questionnaires (see Table 2) usable for data analyses.

Participating institutions	Number of completed questionnaires
Nelson Mandela Metropolitan University	56
University of Pretoria	60
Walter Sisulu University	222
Tshwane University of Technology	103
Central University of Technology	50
North West University	119
Total number of questionnaires	610

Tab. 2: Distribution and number of questionnaires

Data were analysed by means of SPSS and the effect sizes were calculated to explore the differences between race groups regarding the factors influencing travel choices.

4.   Results

The results consist of two sections – a comparison of the demographic profile and travel behaviour of black and white tourism students and, secondly, effect sizes to indicate the differences between the race and factors influencing destination choice.

4.1   Comparison of the demographic profile of black and white tourism students

It is clear from Table 3 that more females participated in the study. It is a general trend in South Africa that more females study tourism. It is interesting to note that the black students are older than the white students, which might be due to various factors. Due to the geographic location of the universities, most black students were from the Eastern Cape and most white students were from Gauteng.

Attribute	Percent: Black students N = 371 (60%)	Percent: White students N = 239 (40%)
Gender:		
Male	20%	8%
Female	40%	32%
Age:		
18-21 years of age	30%	28%
22-25 years of age	27%	11%
26-30 years of age	3%	1%
Province of residence:		
Gauteng	8%	16%
Mpumalanga	1%	2%
North West	2%	6%
Free State	5%	6%
Eastern Cape	37%	4%
Western Cape	0.2%	1%
Northern Cape	0.5%	1%
KwaZulu-Natal	1%	2%
Limpopo	4%	1%
Outside RSA	1%	0.3%

Tab. 3: Demographic profile of black and white tourism students

Race		Relatives	Holiday home	Camping	Chalets	Guest-house	Hotel
Black	Count	208	57	12	18	23	61
	% of Total	71.0%	41.0%	12.5%	26.5%	50.0%	55.0%
White	Count	85	82	84	50	23	50
	% of Total	29.0%	59.0%	87.5%	73.5%	50.0%	45.0%
Total	Count	293	139	96	68	46	111
	% of Total	100.0%	100.0%	100.0%	100.0%	100.0%	100.0%

Tab. 4: Cross-tabulation between race and accommodation preferences

Race		Car	Bus	Taxi	Motorcycle	Aeroplane	Train
Black	Count	163	144	66	0	24	4
	% of Total	41.8%	90.0%	93.0%	0%	25.8%	50.0%
White	Count	227	16	5	3	69	4
	% of Total	58.2%	10.0%	7.0%	100.0%	74.2%	50.0%
Total	Count	390	160	71	3	93	8
	% of Total	100.0%	100.0%	100.0%	100.0%	100.0%	100.0%

Tab. 5: Cross-tabulation between race and transport preferences

Car as a mode of transport seems to be popular with both race groups. However, a higher percentage of white students prefer to travel by car and the black students make use of a variety of transport modes, including cars, buses and taxis.

Weekend-trips

The following section focuses on a discussion of the different types of trips that can be undertaken, including weekend-trips (2 nights), holidays and overseas trips.

Race		Number of weekend trips						Total
		1	2	3	4	5	6	
Black	Count	26	69	89	65	48	56	353
	% of Total	4.4%	11.7%	15.0%	11.0%	8.1%	9.5%	59.6%
White	Count	5	32	60	53	36	53	239
	% of Total	.8%	5.4%	10.1%	9.0%	6.1%	9.0%	40.4%
Total	Count	31	101	149	118	84	109	592
	% of Total	5.2%	17.1%	25.2%	19.9%	14.2%	18.4%	100.0%

Tab. 6: Number of weekend trips

Race		Visit Family	Visit friends	For pleasure	Attend special events
Black	Count	203	63	95	37
	% of Total	68.8%	48.1%	42.8%	39.8%
White	Count	92	68	127	56
	% of Total	31.2%	51.9%	57.2%	60.2%
Total	Count	295	131	222	93
	% of Total	100.0%	100.0%	100.0%	100.0%

Tab. 7: Reasons for travelling on weekend trips

Black and white students indicated that they take three weekend trips per year, although it is clear that black students, in general, take more weekend trips than white students. Black students go on weekend trips to visit family, which has implications for the tourism industry. White students, however, indicated a preference for pleasure although visiting family was also considered as important.

Holidays

According to Table 8, both black and white students go on 2-3 holidays per year but black students tend to go on more holidays than white students. Black students also consider travelling to their family for longer than a weekend as a holiday and some may even regard travelling home as a holiday. It is, however, clear that students have time available to travel when considering the number of weekend trips and holidays. Both race groups indicated relaxation as the main motivator to go on holiday (Table 9).

Race		Holidays					Total
		Number per year					
		1	2 - 3	4 - 5	> 5	Never	1
Black	Count	99	162	51	35	13	360
	% of Total	16.6%	27.2%	8.6%	5.9%	2.2%	60.4%
White	Count	89	111	26	7	3	236
	% of Total	14.9%	18.6%	4.4%	1.2%	.5%	39.6%
Total	Count	188	273	77	42	16	596
	% of Total	31.5%	45.8%	12.9%	7.0%	2.7%	100.0%

Tab. 8: Number of holidays

Race		Escape daily routine	Meet new people	Relaxation	To enjoy the company of friends	Adventure & sport
Black	Count	51	74	154	79	30
	% of Total	34.5%	79.6%	47.7%	58.5%	44.8%
White	Count	97	19	169	56	37
	% of Total	65.5%	20.4%	52.3%	41.5%	55.2%
Total	Count	148	93	323	135	67
	% of Total	100.0%	100.0%	100.0%	100.0%	100.0%

Tab. 9: Reasons for going on holiday

Travelling overseas

Travelling overseas is not popular or, maybe, most of the time not possible or affordable. Most black students have never travelled overseas and, whilst most white students indicated similar results, more white students tend to travel overseas. When travelling overseas it is only once a year. Even with affordable travel packages it is still expensive for South African students to travel overseas whilst European and American Students have more opportunities in this regard. When travelling overseas it is mainly for holiday reasons, although a number of the students travel for work-related reasons (Table 10 and 11).

Race		Number of trips per year				Total
		1	2 - 3	4 - 5	Never	1
Black	Count	35	4	1	297	337
	% of Total	6.1%	.7%	.2%	51.8%	58.8%
White	Count	56	4	0	176	236
	% of Total	9.8%	.7%	.0%	30.7%	41.2%
Total	Count	91	8	1	473	573
	% of Total	15.9%	1.4%	.2%	82.5%	100.0%

Tab. 10: Number of overseas trips

Race		Holiday	Work	Study	Visit family & friends	To observe other lifestyles
Black	Count	30	28	14	17	47
	% of Total	34.9%	57.1%	73.7%	41.5%	67.1%
White	Count	56	21	5	24	23
	% of Total	65.1%	42.9%	26.3%	58.5%	32.9%
Total	Count	86	49	19	41	70
	% of Total	100.0%	100.0%	100.0%	100.0%	100.0%

Tab. 11: Reasons for going overseas

4.2 Factors influencing Destination Choice

A one-way analysis of variance (ANOVA) was conducted to explore the impact of the variables: *race* on the various factors influencing destination choice. Ellis and Steyn (2003) state that a natural way to comment on practical significance is by using the absolute difference between the groups (for example race: (1) and (2)) divided by the square root of the mean square error. This measure is called an effect size, which not only makes the difference independent of units and sample size, but also relates it to the spread of the data (Steyn, 1999 & Steyn, 2000, as quoted by Ellis and Steyn (2003).

Cohen (as quoted by Ellis & Steyn, 2003) gives the following guidelines for the interpretation of the effect size in the current article:

- Small effect: $d = 0.2$
- Medium effect: $d = 0.5$ and
- Large effect: $d = 0.8$.

Data with $d \geq 0.8$ as practically significant, since it is the result of a difference having a large effect.

		N	Mean	Std. deviation	Std. Error	95% Confidence interval for mean		Effect size
						Lower bound	Upper bound	
Traditions	Black	310	2.77	.987	.056	2.66	2.88	
	White	236	1.97	.735	.048	1.88	2.06	0.80
Sports facilities	Black	308	2.51	1.023	.058	2.40	2.62	
	White	236	1.90	.812	.053	1.80	2.01	0.61
Modern facilities	Black	301	3.20	.821	.047	3.11	3.29	
	White	235	2.60	.827	.054	2.50	2.71	0.60

Tab. 12: Factors influencing destination choices: Large to medium practical significant differences

It is clear from Table 12 that white and black students differ concerning certain factors, and that small to large differences exist. Firstly, there is a large practical significant difference with regard to the influence of traditions on travel decisions (0.80). Black students regard traditions as a more important influencing factor than white students. Secondly, there are medium practical significant differences with regard to the importance of sports facilities (0.61) and modern facilities (0.60).

In both cases the black students considered these factors more important in travel decision making than white students.

		N	Mean	Std. Deviation	Std. Error	95% Confidence Interval for Mean		Effect size
						Lower Bound	Upper Bound	
Entertainment	Black	310	3.51	.705	.040	3.43	3.59	
	White	236	3.03	.830	.054	2.93	3.14	0.48
Popularity	Black	301	2.92	.972	.056	2.81	3.03	
	White	235	2.45	.892	.058	2.33	2.56	0.47
Parents' influence	Black	309	2.60	1.069	.061	2.48	2.72	
	White	235	2.21	.931	.061	2.09	2.33	0.39
Climate	Black	306	3.31	.867	.050	3.21	3.41	
	White	236	2.96	.822	.053	2.86	3.07	0.35
Distance	Black	309	2.77	1.034	.059	2.65	2.88	
	White	236	2.43	.850	.055	2.32	2.54	0.34
Peaceful surroundings	Black	315	3.17	.941	.053	3.06	3.27	
	White	236	2.87	.851	.055	2.76	2.98	0.30
Security	Black	306	3.70	.590	.034	3.63	3.77	
	White	236	3.45	.710	.046	3.36	3.54	0.25
Beautiful nature	Black	328	3.40	.731	.040	3.32	3.48	
	White	236	3.20	.715	.047	3.11	3.30	0.20
Accommodation	Black	308	3.47	.780	.044	3.39	3.56	
	White	234	3.28	.755	.049	3.18	3.38	0.19
Low cost	Black	311	3.05	.967	.055	2.95	3.16	
	White	234	2.91	.800	.052	2.81	3.01	0.14
Activities	Black	299	3.33	.734	.042	3.25	3.42	
	White	236	3.19	.732	.048	3.09	3.28	0.14
Value for money	Black	306	3.46	.751	.043	3.37	3.54	
	White	235	3.59	.542	.035	3.52	3.66	0.13
Beaches	Black	308	2.96	.958	.055	2.85	3.07	
	White	236	3.04	.844	.055	2.93	3.15	0.08

Tab. 13: Factors influencing destination choices: Small practical significant differences

It is clear from Table 13 that small practical significant differences exist between white and black students regarding the factors indicated above. Firstly, there are small practical significant differences with regard to entertainment, popularity of the destination, the influence of parents, climate, distance to the destination and peaceful surroundings. In all the cases, the black students consider these factors as more important than the white students although they all agree on their importance.

No practical significant differences were found between black and white students regarding security, beautiful nature, accommodation, low cost, activities, value for money and the availability of beaches. Secondly, white students consider the availability of beaches as more important than the black students.

5. Implications and Recommendations

Based on the results and findings of the research conducted, the following implications can be identified:

Firstly, results indicated differences in the travel behaviour of students based on race. Therefore, when developing marketing strategies for black students it is recommended that marketers develop packages that include transport and accommodation. On the other hand, it is recommended that self-drive packages are developed for white students.

Secondly, it was found that black students travel to relatives over weekends. Based on this finding, it is important to develop more awareness programmes of local travel opportunities such as *Short Left (A tourism awareness television programme)*, as students may not be aware of what South Africa has to offer for students as tourists.

Thirdly, since differences exist in terms of factors influencing destination choice, it is recommended that marketing messages focus on the needs of the particular market, such as sports facilities for black students.

Fourthly, the results indicated that aspects such as security, accommodation, low costs and so on are important for both black and white students. These aspects should therefore be taken into consideration when doing product planning.

6. Conclusions

The purpose of this research was to compare the travel behaviour of black and white tourism students from selected universities in South Africa. The contribution of the research is as follows:

Firstly, the results revealed differences and similarities in the travel behaviour of black and white tourism students concerning the accommodation and transport preferences of students. Black students prefer to stay with relatives and white students make use of a variety of accommodation options. In terms of transport, it can be concluded that black students make use of a variety of transport options whilst white students travel by car.

Secondly, the results revealed differences in terms of type of travel. It was found that black students go on more weekend trips than white students, although both groups go on three weekend trips per year on average. Black students travel on weekend trips to visit family whilst white students travel mainly for pleasure. Concerning holidays, both groups take 2 3 holidays per year mainly to relax. Travelling patterns with regard to overseas trips differ. A large number of black students have not been overseas, but those that go overseas travel for holiday and work purposes. Similarly, a large number of white students have not been overseas but those that have been overseas travel for holiday purposes.

Thirdly, differences were found in terms of the factors influencing destination choice. Traditions, sports facilities and modern facilities are more important influential factors for black students than for white students. Although smaller in effect, black students are more influenced by entertainment, popularity of the destination, the influence of parents, climate, distance to the destination, and peaceful surroundings than white students.

Fourthly, the results revealed that both groups consider security, beautiful nature, accommodation, low cost, activities, value for money and beaches as important when make destination choices. These factors can therefore be seen as universal.

Results also confirmed similarities among the two groups such as the importance of low costs, adequate accommodation, and activities. This research is useful in product development as well as in the development of marketing strategies. It is, however, important to continue this type of research as trends change and the influence of race and/or culture may also change over time.

References

BÖHLER, S., GRISCHKAT, S., HAUSTEIN, S. & HUNECKE, M. 2005. Encouraging environmentally sustainable holiday travel. *Transportation Research*, 40(8): 652-670.

CARR, N. 2002. Going with the flow: an assessment of the relationship between young people's leisure and vacation behaviour. *Tourism Geographies*, 4(2): 115-134.

CARR, N. 2003. The tourist experience. *Journal of Sustainable Tourism*, 11(5): 455-457.

CARR, N. 2005. Sightseeing: an integral component of the study abroad experience. *Tourism*, 53(1): 77-83.

DELLAERT, B.G.C., ETTEMA, D.F. & LINDH, C. 1998. *Tourism Management*, 19(4):313-328.

ELLIS, S. & STEYN, H.S. 2003. Management dynamics. *Contemporary Research*, 12(4):51-53.

GALLARZA, M.G. & SAURA, I.G. 2006. Value dimensions, perceived value, satisfaction and loyalty: An investigation of university students' travel behaviour. *Tourism Management*, 27(3): 437-452.

GOODHALL, B. & ASHWORTH, G. 1988. Marketing in the tourism industry. United Kingdom: Croom Helm.

HARVEY, K. 2005. Travelling light. SAWUBONA, June 2005.

HEUNG, V.C.S., QU, H. AND CHU, R. 2001. The relationship between vacation factors and socio-demographic and travelling characteristics: the case of Japanese leisure travellers. *Tourism Management*, 22(3): 259-269

HOBSON, J.S. & JOSIAM, B. 1992. Spring break student travel – an exploratory study. *Journal of Tourism and Travel Management*, 1(3): 87-97.

HSU, C.H.C. & SUNG, S. 1997. Travel behaviour of international students. *Journal of Travel Research*, 36(1): 59.

HSU, C.H.C & KANG, S.K. 2001. Segmenting travel information centre visitors by vacation decision-making. Kowloon: Hong Kong.

KOTZE, F. 2005. The role of print media in travel decision making. Potchefstroom: North West University. (Dissertation – MA.)

McKETCHER, B., WONG, C & LAU, G. 2006. How tourists consume a destination. *Journal of Business Research*, 59(5): 647-652.

MICHAEL, I, ARMSTRONG, A. & KING, B. 2003. The travel behaviour of international students: The relationship between studying abroad and their choice of student destinations. *Journal of Vacation Management*, 10(1): 57-66.

OPPERMAN, M. 1995. Travel Life Cycle. *Annals of Tourism Research*, 22(3): 535-552.

PATKOSE, M., STOKES, A.M. & COOK, S.D. 2005. Leisure travel planning: How consumers make travel decisions. TIA Report.

PEARCE, P. & SON, A. 2004. Youth tourism markets in Australia: Comparing the travel behaviours of international English language students and backpackers. *Tourism*, 52(4): 341-349.

PIZAM, A. & SUSSMANN, S. 1995. Does nationality affect tourism behaviour? *Annals of Tourism Research*, 22(4): 901-917.

REISINGER, Y. AND TURNER, L.W. 2003. Cross-cultural behaviour in tourism: concepts and analysis. Oxford: Butterworth-Heinemann.

SAAYMAN, M. 2000. En route with tourism. 2nd ed. Potchefstroom: Institute for Tourism and Leisure Studies.

SAAYMAN, M. 2001. Tourism marketing in South Africa. 2nd ed. Potchefstroom: Leisure Consultants and Publications.

SCHRAGE, C., VAN EEDEN, S. & SHOHAM, A. 2001. Leisure travel by students: a three-country study. Paper presented at the 2001 World Marketing Congress, Cardiff, Wales. 28 June-1 July 2001.

SHOHAM, A., SCHRAGE, C. & VAN EEDEN, S. 2004. Student travel behaviour: a cross-national study. *Journal of Travel and Tourism Marketing*, 17(4): 1-10.

TAL, G. & HANDY, S. 2005. The travel behaviour of immigrants and race/ethnic groups: an analysis of the 2001 national household transportation survey. California: Institute of Transportation Studies.

UM, S. & CROMPTON, J.L. 1990. Attitude determinations in tourism destination choice. *Annals of Tourism Research*, 17(3): 432-448.

YAU, O.H.M. & CHAN, C.F. 1990. Hong Kong as a travel destination in South-East Asia: A multidimensional approach. *Tourism Management*, 11(2): 123-132.

ZMUD, J.P. & ARCE, C.H. 1998. Influence of consumer culture and race on travel behaviour. NuStats International: 379-389.

El Día de los Muertos: A Mexican Tradition

Charyn López

1. Introduction

El Día de los Muertos, literally: the day of the dead, is a Mexican tradition that has been celebrated since Pre-Hispanic days and continues to this day. This festivity has many aspects depending on the culture and the region of the Mexican Republic where it is celebrated. Every year it takes place on the first two days of the month of November, a date on which a special celebration is held and gifts are offered up for all those who have gone from this life to continue on their way towards salvation.

Even though the attitude towards death is pivotal to the Mexicans, with the passage of time, this celebration has lost its real meaning, that is why we, who are in charge of passing on our customs and traditions, must preserve the real meaning and emphasize the importance of El Día de los Muertos, using our cultural tourism as a tool.

Sadly, we can affirm that El Día de los Muertos is slowly dying. This may sound like a play on words, although this phrase is full of meaning for us, the Mexicans. This tradition is being buried in the past, and if we do not do something and do not try to promote this celebration, it will become no more than a memory for the Mexican people.

We must ask ourselves why this custom is being forgotten. There are many answers to this, and I could give you a long list, but I will only underline three factors that I consider to be of great importance.

Firstly, we are strongly influenced by our neighbors to the north, the United States; it is really surprising to see the way in which their traditions have infiltrated the Mexican culture rapidly and deeply. As an example we can mention Valentine's Day, Santa Claus and worst of all Halloween. This festivity is largely responsible for slowly but surely "burying" our Día de los Muertos. In rural areas, many people can still be seen in the cemeteries, and altars to the dead are set up inside houses, with offerings of objects that were cherished by the loved ones that have gone before us. On the other hand, in larger or more cosmopolitan cities like the Federal District, Monterrey or Guadalajara, the "Orange Pumpkin" has taken the place of the traditional Cempasuchil flower.

Secondly, we cannot close our eyes to globalization and ignore its impact, for just as it has benefited or harmed our economy, technology and day to day life, globalization has also impacted the heart of our country, its traditions and customs. However, the question must be asked: Why choose Halloween instead of El Día de los Muertos? What does this American festivity have that is not present in the Mexican one? Could it simply be the result of aggressive marketing?

Thirdly, we lack knowledge of this celebration. Who is to blame for this: Our grandparents, our parents, school, or the media? It is in fact our own fault. We are more interested in foreign customs and lose sight of our own roots. An example of this is how many children wait expectantly for the night of October 31st, to go out into the streets, knocking on neighbors' doors chanting "trick or treat". It is really strange to see streets full of children dressed as Casper, Pumpkin or Morticia. However, when these same children hear that others come out on the 1st or 2nd of November asking for the "Calaverita" or "Su Muerto", they are confused, yet no one can explain it to them. They have become accustomed to Halloween, so El Día de los Muertos has no meaning for them.

Despite all this, el Día de los Muertos is one of the celebrations that best illustrate Mexican culture; we celebrate death with courage and bravery, a theme which is taboo in other cultures. In his book "The Labyrinth of Solitude" the great Octavio Paz wrote "…the inhabitants of New York, Paris or London never uttered the word 'Death', because it burned their lips. Mexicans on the other hand, say it often, they make fun of it, they caress it, sleep with it, celebrate it, it is one of their favorite toys, and a long lasting love".

This is because, since ancient times, man has felt the necessity, indeed an urge to explain many things to himself, death amongst others.

"Ever since he appeared on earth, man has found a series of questions and phenomena that he does not fully understand, that are beyond his understanding; because of this he has looked for explanations that allow him to organize what happens around him. He has elaborated many answers that go from the magical-religious to the scientific that give meaning to his life and to the phenomenon that surround it, and that have given origin to myths, religions and science. Among the mysteries that surround man's existence, the fundamentals of live and death have been constant, the same as the ones that derive from them; the destiny of matter and the soul, the possibility of another time, the desire to transcend in space and time".[1]

Thus in our country, the indigenous cultures and the Spanish tradition blended to give origin to one of the most ancient and fundamental festivities of our nation: El Día de los Muertos.

It is necessary to first understand the origin of this festivity and later to focus on one of the states where this tradition is most deeply rooted and has been kept intact.

2. The origin of the Día de los Muertos

To fully understand the real meaning of the celebration of El Día de los Muertos, it is necessary to know a little about its origin and fully appreciate its importance as a Mexican tradition.

The origin of this celebration is as old as is the existence of man on earth; since man first appeared he has been confronted with a series of questions and phenomena that he cannot easily understand, they were beyond his comprehension, for which he has looked for explanations to help him understand what happens around him. He has found different answers based on religion, magic or science; all of which have given meaning to life and the phenomena that surround him.

Since ancient times, man has felt the need, the obsession and the urge to explain many things, death among others.

As has been mentioned, Mexicans have their very own way of looking at death and in some way dominating it. Xavier Villaurrutia said: "Here, we have a great affinity with death which has a stronger attraction due to the amount of Indian blood that we have in our veins. The more Creole we are, the bigger the fear of death, since that is what we have been taught".

"In Mexico the customs associated with death and the funerary ceremonies are ancient traditions that have become central elements of our ritual life, and of the identity of the Mexican people. The Mexican expressions of death, be it in popular art, festivities, food, sweets, every day life or in celebration mockery have attracted attention everywhere, since in most countries, mainly of the first world, all reference to death is looked upon with fear and denial and kept at a distance. In Mexico the

---

[1] ZARAUZ, Héctor; *La fiesta de la muerte*. México: CONACULTA; 2004.

festivity of El Día de los Muertos finds expression in all areas of cultural life including for example hand-crafts, music and food."[2]

It is worth mentioning that Mexico today is a product of crossbreeding, not only racial but also gastronomical, in the language and in culture that encompasses all traditions.

Since Pre-Hispanic time celebrations for the dead, offerings, and sacrifices to the gods, as well as to the deceased have taken place.

"Archeological excavations were found in Tlapacoya dating from the year 1350 b.C. which show the origins of the funerary cults in Mexico. Tombs with the remains of bent bodies, sumptuous offerings and also possible human sacrifices were discovered. The bodies dating from the period between 1300 and 800 b.C. appeared to be swaddled in 'petates' and cotton blankets, with pottery, ornaments, food, drinks and personal objects. If they were children, there were toys and sometimes sacrificed dogs. This burials show certain developments in the Pre-Hispanic cultures. Towards the year 200 b.C. the burials become more elaborate, tombs have stone walls, and body cremation in Teotihuacan." [3]

Even though throughout Mexico, there are a great number of cultures that celebrate el Día de los Muertos, it is the Aztecs whose rites and funerary traditions stand out.

It has become evident from archeological excavations of tombs and consecrated sites that in Pre-Hispanic funerary, ritual burials held a special place. For example the custom of offerings in burials dates back to the early pre-classic age; in places such as Tlapacoya, Cuicuilco and Tlatilco. Later during the classic age, large ceremonial centers like Teotihuacan in the central plateau, Monte Alban in Oaxaca, Tajin in the Gulf, Tikal and Palenque in the Mayan area, burials and tombs acquired monumental dimensions.

Among the Aztecs if the burial was of an important person, the body was wrapped in feathers and blankets, two or four live slaves were buried with him, they carried their grinding stones to make his meals while he was on the way to the underworld, they also took food and riches according to his rank.

The same burials had offerings with objects that the deceased had used during his life or the ones he might need on his way to the

---

[2] Íbidem.
[3] Íbidem.

underworld. We find cups, pots, stones, bird bones or ornaments like obsidian ear spools and on some occasions, coral and conches to recreate the underworld ambiance.

The offerings we know today have their real origin in these times, since the Mesoamerican civilizations also made offerings to their deceased. Towards the years 1200 to 500 b.C. funerary rites became more important, as people's ideas about the afterworld developed and they took greater care of what and how many objects they gave them.

3. The Spanish contribution to El Día de los Muertos

With the arrival of the Spaniards the festivity became richer, more elaborate; crossbreeding started and this was reflected in different aspects of daily life such as gastronomy, physiognomy, forms of speech and of course in traditions.

It is because of this, that the celebration of the dead suffered a series of changes. Pre-Hispanic and Spanish elements have blended, resulting in a very distinct way of celebrating this festivity in Mexico. Priests had the mission of Christianizing the people and a phenomenon known as religious syncretism, where two cosmovisions or cultures unite and form a third one, emerged. Zarauz said:

"What Christianity intended then, was to superimpose religious elements, and the priests combined pagan rites with catholic ceremonies. The most graphic and tangible of these are found in the buildings of churches, on top of the remains of indigenous temples, like in Oaxaca where the catholic church of Mitla is built over the Zapotec ruins".

4. Festivity of El Día de los Muertos in Oaxaca

Since there are different ways of celebrating El Día de los Muertos within Mexico, I would like to look into how it is celebrated in Oaxaca, since here its Pre-Hispanic roots are kept alive, even though the Spanish influence is evident in their customs and traditions.

In order to understand the nuances that characterize the Día de los Muertos in Oaxaca, I would like to provide some details about this wonderful state in the south east of Mexico.

4.1 Oaxaca

Mexico is a vast territory embodying several cultures and forms of life, even though there are states that are known for either, their customs, traditions, gastronomy or history, Oaxaca encompasses them all.

"The state of Oaxaca is one of the thirty-two federal entities of Mexico, it is in the southern part of the country, on the extreme south east of the Tehuantepec isthmus, it borders with the state of Guerrero to the west, Puebla on the northeast, Veracruz to the north and Chiapas to the east. It has 600 kilometers of coast on the Pacific Ocean. Because of its extension it is the fifth state of the country and holds 4.8% of the total surface. It has a rich multicultural composition where more than 16 ethnic groups live together. The same as in other states of the federation, Oaxaca has a constitution, a code of laws, and its own coat of arms.

The name comes from the Nahuatl Huāxyacac imposed by the Aztecs in the XV century, when it was incorporated into the Tenochca empire. Huāx means in Spanish 'huaje', a plant of the valley region, Yaca, literally means nose, the suffix C is equivalent to Tepec, that means place, in an abbreviated form. Phonetically the glyph would be read as 'Huax yaca tepec' 'on the tip of the huajes'. A linguistic transformation into Spanish results in the actual Oaxaca".[4]

The state of Oaxaca has seen great tragedies, continuous battles and a cultural, economic and social divide, from the arrival of the Spaniards until today.

The state of Oaxaca is one of the most distinctive states in Mexico, mainly because of its famous gastronomy. It has a wide range of natural resources, spectacular landscape and the inheritance of Pre-Hispanic culture as well as colonial architecture.

Its culture is rich, since the 14 different indigenous groups that live there keep their customs and traditions alive. From a culinary point of view, Oaxaca has many well-known dishes ranging from simple soups that contain traditional condiments and chilies, to "mole" which is a traditional and sophisticated dish because of the variety of ingredients it includes, and the way it is prepared.

The cuisine is based mainly on Pre-Hispanic dishes which absorbed the influence of Spanish foods and ingredients. The traditional ingredients are: corn, beans, tomatoes, tomatillos and a great variety of chilies. We also find many plants that are used to complement and enrich

---

[4] s/a. Consultado el día 7 de noviembre de 2007 en:
http://es.wikipedia.org/wiki/Oaxaca.

the flavor of food, like: nopal, chepil and rabbit herbs, hierba santa, verdolaga and epazote.

Mexico's most important contribution to international gastronomy is probably cocoa. Even though cocoa is originally from the state of Tabasco, it is cultivated in the tropical regions of Oaxaca, and used quite inventively in their cuisine. Cocoa is used to make chocolate, Popo and tejate, Pre-Hispanic beverages originally called "beverages of the gods" which are still being used traditionally as part of the festivities of the state.

"Oaxaca gastronomy is as vast as its territory, which is composed of 7 regions: Los Valles Centrales, La Cañada, Tuxtepec, La Costa, La Mixteca, La Sierra y El Istmo. Each region has specific products as well as specific way of cooking them, thus developing a wide variety of dishes".[5]

Today inside the representative gastronomy of Oaxaca we can find: tlayudas, tamales, tejate, huarachitos, totopos, empanadas, Oaxaca cheese, mezcal, pinole, "pan de muerto", chocolate and seven kinds of mole: black, red, yellow, green, chichilo, with almonds and stewed. It is also one of the states where the largest variety of insects is eaten. The tourist portal of Oaxaca offers the following description of its gastronomy:

"Para comer en Oaxaca, ni ganas se necesitan. Con la comida oaxaqueña, el gusto entra por ojos, nariz y garganta; pero si alguien no lo creyera, todo es cuestión de abrirle el apetito.

Y para abrir el apetito que tal una copita de mezcal, y aquí que si el refrán aquel de que 'para todo mal, mezcal y para todo bien también' no es oaxaqueño debería serlo, a juzgar por la pulimenta que han alcanzado los artesanos de este agave sensacional.

Mezcal aparte, un bocadillo que más vale apenas probar, para no quedarse sin los guisos fuertes de después. Chapulines doraditos, empanadas de amarillo, salsita de gusanos de maguey, totopos, quesillo, chorizo bien frito o memela con asiento.

De la mesa regional y ya para entrar en calor, lo más probable es que el estómago sea estimulado con un buen caldo de guías de calabaza, espinazo hecho en tomate, mole en todas sus variedades: amarillo, coloradito, verde, almendrado y chichilo, incluyendo mole negro, que merece probada aparte.

Además de los moles, imposible hacerle el feo al estofado o unos chiles rellenos y

---

[5] TRILLING, Susana. *Seasons of my heart. A culinary journey through Oaxaca.* EUA: Ballantine Books; 1999.

para completar unos tamales en hoja de plátano.

Claro que ello no evita el que de pronto aparezcan por allí una sopa de ejotes con chepil, o de garbanzo y frijol tostado y molido, un caldillo de nopales, continuados con otros moles, tal vez el manchamantel o el coloradito.

Y para que tanto bocado no se atore en la garganta, las bebidas se multiplican al mejor gusto.

Con el chocolate, rigurosamente molido en metate, como debe ser, y agua o leche, queda un espumoso brebaje que puede ser ingerido frío o caliente.

Hay también unas aguas de Casilda, que no son filtro de brujería para el amor, sino para quitar la sed, y que se hacen de horchata con tuna y nueces, de chía, de limón rallado, etc.

Y si de postres se trata, aquí no hay pero que valga. Si la gloria está en los cielos, la repostería de Oaxaca es uno de sus anticipos. No en vano adquirieron gran refinamiento en los conventos. En el colmo de la gula, para acabar de demostrar la finura de sensibilidad, la delicadeza cultural del alma oaxaqueña, están las nieves vueltas sorbete o leche quemada con tuna."[6]

As we can see, the gastronomy in Oaxaca is as varied and extreme as Susan Trilling's book, which presents all the recipes of the state on more than 600 pages.

The gastronomy of the state is related directly to the festivities, one of the most important ones being the celebrations of el Día de los Muertos that can only be surpassed by the "Guelaguetza".

4.2 El Día de los Muertos in Oaxaca

We know that death has been celebrated in Mexico since time immemorial. Therefore this tradition is deeply rooted in the spiritual life of the Mexicans. The traditions and rituals have been kept alive thanks to the indigenous people.

On the other hand, the violent clash of the indigenous cultures and the Spaniards shaped every aspect of their personal experience. Since then, a long process of crossbreeding of customs, rites and Cosmo visions has generated new perceptions.

In the ceremonies dedicated to the dead, the intermingling of these two visions propitiated the surge of a celebration full of mysticism and memories, founding a new festive character with expressions full of

---

[6] sa. Consultado el día 7 de noviembre de 2007 en:
http://www.gooaxaca.com/traditions/gastronomia.html.

color, flavors and textures, manifested in food, hand crafts, flowers and rites, that, after centuries we continue doing today.

Zarauz says in his book "The Feast of the Dead": "Oaxaca is one of the states with the strongest presence and diversity of indigenous population; it is probably the most pluriethnic of the whole country and because of this, celebrating the dead acquires a heterogeneous character."

The celebration of the Dead in Oaxaca is very old and according to Friar Jose Antonio Gay, is similar to the actual festivity. For the occasion turkeys were killed, tamales were prepared, and were offered on an altar. Upon nightfall people gathered around the altar to pray to their gods and ask them for health, good crops, and prosperity. All through the night no one lifted their eyes for fear of offending the dead, since they could be punished for it.

Jose Antonio Gay describes in his history of Oaxaca the traditions and customs around El Día de los Muertos:

"The cult to the dead did not end in the grave. In addition to the anniversary that each one celebrated, (…) had the custom of making a scaffold or catafalque covered with black veils, over which flowers and fruits were placed and around which they prayed to honor their dead. They also had a common commemoration of the dead that for some reason coincided with the one Catholics celebrated. The indigenous people prepared themselves for this celebration by killing a great number of turkeys or other birds which they hunted and made many other dishes like tamales (petlaltmali), mole or totomoli. These dishes were placed on a table or altar and when night arrived, all the members of the family sat or stood around the altar, they held a wake praying to the gods asking them to intercede and grant them health, good crops and prosperity. All through the night they did not dare to raise their eyes for fear that if they did, and one of the dead was eating one of the dishes, the dead would feel affronted and ashamed and would send great punishments to the living. The next morning the living would congratulate each other for having paid their dues and the dishes were handed out to the poor and strangers, if there weren't any the dishes would be thrown into occult places; the dead had already extracted the nutrients leaving them empty and without any juice, and by touching the dishes had made them sacred." [7]

Today, these traditions have not changed much since they have been guarded mainly by the indigenous people of the state. That is why big cities do not celebrate El Día de los Muertos, only the small

---

[7] GAY, José Antonio. *Historia de Oaxaca*. México: Edit. Porrúa; 2006.

communities where traditions are handed down from generation to generation.

In the city of Oaxaca the celebration begins on the 31st of October and goes as follows; families build the altar to the dead inside their homes or in the cemeteries, cempasuchil flowers, candles, beverages and an arch made of reeds are a must, the same as the famous bread of the dead. It is said that the candles must be lit when the souls of the dead arrive.

On the night of the 1st of November, there is a dance to scare away the dead and help their souls come back to where they belong. The dance consists of a parade of people in costumes with masks, they have music and they make up speeches, the main characters of the dance group are death, the devil, the widow, the doctor, the foreman or boss, the priest, the altar boy, the witch and the grandparents. The dance group visits several homes and asks for their "muerto" which consists of food and drink.

Fig. 1: The Comparsa (a special dance of these days)

On the 2nd of November the day is dedicated to all the saints meaning to all the dead.

From the end of the month of October, families buy all the products they will use as offerings at the market; Cempasuchil flower, a red flower "mano de leon", candles, apples, guavas, bread and beverages. The altar is built in one of the rooms of the house and must be ready by 31st October. Yellow beef tamales, fish and prawns as well as flowers, religious images and candles, sugar flowers and bread angel faces are all placed on the altar and the air is fragrant with incense and copal. On 1st

November people go out onto the streets and invite friends and relatives to join in; once gathered, they remember the dead.

It is a common custom that on these days the famous musical bands of the region play in churches and in the graveyards which have been cleaned and adorned with Cempasuchil flowers and candles.

It is worth mentioning that all over Oaxaca there are different forms of celebrating the Dia de Los Muertos, but they still have the same ancient origin.

In order to understand all the elements that are found on an altar, it is necessary to analyze each one.

5. Elements on an Altar to the Dead

There are eight elements on an Altar to the dead:

1. **Water:** is the fountain of life, it is offered to the spirits, so that they can quench their thirst after their long voyage and be fortified for their return. In some cultures it symbolizes the purity of the soul.
2. **Salt:** is the purifying element, used so that the body will not be corrupted.
3. **Ocote (a kind of wood):** (today mostly candles are used) the flame it produces means light, faith, and hope. It is the guide so that the souls can reach their old homes and it also lights the journey back.
4. **Copal or incense:** it is the element that enhances prayer and praise. The fragrance helps to cleanse bad spirits.
5. **Flowers:** symbols of festivity.
6. **Petate:** a straw sleeping mat, used also as a table and as a shroud.
7. **Dog:** helps the souls cross the river.
8. **Food:** permits this celebration to be festive.

La Huesuda, La Calaca, La Catrina, who all represent death, are the main character of this day and cannot be absent.

Although several questions remain still to be answered, we must recognize that El Día de los Muertos is the crown jewel of Mexican culture and must be kept alive.

References

ARGUETA, Jermán. *Crónicas y leyendas mexicanas. Día de muertos*, México: Crónicas y leyendas; 2007.

ESPARZA, Manuel. *The Founding of the City of Oaxaca.* México: INAH; 1993.

GAY, José Antonio. *Historia de Oaxaca.* México: Edit. Porrúa; 2006

TRILLING, Susana. *Seasons of my heart. A culinary journey through Oaxaca.* EUA: Ballantine Books; 1999.

ZARAUZ, Héctor; *La fiesta de la muerte.* México: CONACULTA; 2004.

s/a. Consultada el día 27 de octubre en:
http://www.oaxaca-mio.com/fiestas/muertos.htm.

s/a. Consultado el día 7 de noviembre de 2007 en:
http://www.gooaxaca.com/traditions/gastronomia.html.

s/a. Consultado el día 7 de noviembre de 2007 en:
http://es.wikipedia.org/wiki/Oaxaca.

Customer-oriented Brand Value Assessment of the German Source Market for the Destination South Africa

Bernd Eisenstein, Alexander Koch

1. Object of investigation

On account of the FIFA World Cup in the summer of 2010 Germans have shown an increased public interest in South Africa, which has been frequently visited by German tourists as a long-haul destination for quite some time. However, so far South Africa has barely been considered to be subject of a touristic survey in Germany.

On the basis of a representative survey, the present study should provide results of the attitude Germans show towards South Africa as a tourist destination regarding the question of how attractive they rate South Africa as a holiday destination and whether they could consider spending their holiday (from one overnight stay) here.

2. Short introduction to the survey

Against this background, empirical baseline data on countries such as Argentina, China, France, Macedonia, Mexico, New Zealand, Norway, Russia, Spain and South Africa which represent the "International Competence Network of Tourism" (ICNT) were surveyed based on 1,000 usable interviews in December 2008 within the scope of the so-called "Destination-Monitor" (DestiMon) by the Institut für Management und Tourismus (IMT) of the Fachhochschule Westküste (West Coast University of Applied Sciences) in Heide/Holstein, Germany. By taking into account those ten travel destinations visited by Germans, the survey provided a broad set of functions to compare. The evaluation was based on a representative online survey of people aged 16 to 64 years living in private households in Germany.

The "market research instrument" DestiMon, applied here, is divided into two parts: One part of it contains a fixed set of questions regarding the travel behaviour of the German speaking population. Therefore, based on cooperation with the GfK-TravelScope team, a representative sample of 20,000 households is being surveyed on a quarterly basis.

Among others, this includes pursuing the long-term objective to establish a scientific forecast system that provides reliable information on the travel behaviour of German citizens. Other parts deal with questions on current issues or, in special surveys, cope with different topics. In the scope of such a special survey, the empirical baseline data on the ICNT member countries as a travel destination for Germans were surveyed in DestiMon.

According to the described objective, the survey focused on the customer-oriented brand value assessment by means of the so-called "four dimensional brand analysis". On the occasion of the "3rd International Tourism Conference" (ITC) held by the university network ICNT in October 2009 at the North-West University, Potchefstroom, South Africa the present article is focused on the results for the destination South Africa.

3. The "four dimensional brand analysis" model – A basic theory

The "four dimensional brand analysis" model materially illustrates the decision-making process when purchasing a product:

The starting point of the model is that "a purchasing decision for a product offered will always be made beginning with the offer itself followed by the consumer's awareness (Ramme 2000, 96)"[1]. Consequently, the provider of a product copes with the challenge to raise the familiarity of the potential consumer by developing product awareness (1. stage), by creating sympathy for the product (2. stage), and by providing willingness to buy the product (3. stage). This model can also be adapted to selecting a travel destination. The provider is successful if his efforts according to the "four dimensional brand analysis" model eventually result in the act of buying (4. stage) and/or in the decision to visit the respective holiday destination (cp. Ramme, ib.).

The presented structure of the "four dimensional brand analysis" model also serves the purpose of rating the customer oriented brand value of conventional products like automobile umbrella brands and

---

[1] Translator's note: roughly translated from the following citation: „… ein angebotenes Produkt immer den Weg vom Angebot über das Bewusstsein [sic!] des Konsumenten bis zur Kaufentscheidung geht …" (Ramme 2000, 96).

fashion brands (cp. Gruner + Jahr AG & Co KG (ed.) 2008, 56), as well as tourist destinations (cp. Eisenstein / Müller / Heubeck 2009). This also was applied in the course of the empirical DestiMon survey, a special survey on the ICNT member countries as a potential tourist destination for Germans.

Figure 1 illustrates the levels of the "four dimensional brand analysis" model applied for travel destinations.

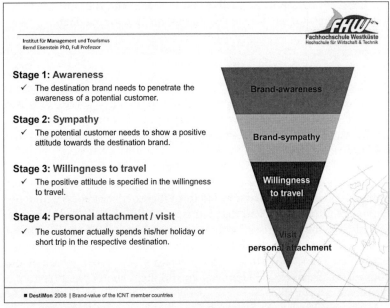

Fig. 1: The "four dimensional brand analysis" model applied for destinations[2]

---

[2] According to: Gruner + Jahr AG & Co KG (ed.) (2001), p. 6.

4. Individual evaluation for South Africa

In the following an individual evaluation for the tourist destination South Africa is presented. Here, the focus is at first on the results in relation to the total amount of interviewees. In addition, selected key results based on socio-demographic segmentations under the aspects of gender, age groups, level of education and heritage (classified by ACNielsen) are emphasized.

As a general remark, the authors point out that possible deviations of 1% between the top-two-box (bottom-two-box) and the sum of all "1" and "2" ratings (of all "4" and "5" ratings) are due to rounding.

4.1 Awareness (1st level)

To determine the popularity of a destination a list containing the mentioned tourist destinations was handed out to the interviewees, in which they had to state whether they are aware of the destination, even if only by the name (assisted brand awareness, 1st level). The result showed that the awareness level of South Africa, as a tourist destination, is 92%, based on the represented German population of the sample.

The authors assume that the FIFA World Cup hosted by South Africa in the summer of 2010 had now led to an increased awareness within the German source market and that this trend is already reflected shown in the relatively high degree of popularity as a tourist destination. Without being capable to compare and thus support this thesis by surveys carried out in past years, the broad media coverage of the event as well as the enthusiasm shared by the Germans for this mega sports event led to the mentioned assumption.

When conducting the aforementioned socio-demographic segmentations, relatively few differences between the respective classes regarding South Africa's level of awareness were surveyed. As a rather clear trend for all investigated travel destinations it could be determined that the level of awareness for the respective target destinations is more pronounced the higher the level of education is. That way the assisted awareness of South Africa as a travel destination varies by the level of education from 86% of the interviewees showing a low level of education to 95% of the interviewees showing a higher level of education and/or graduated from university.

4.2 Level of sympathy (2nd level)

In order to determine the level of sympathy for the destinations the interviewees were asked to what extent on a scale of "1 = very pleasant" to "5 = very unpleasant" they indicate each of the travel destinations.

The average level of sympathy for South Africa as a travel destination is "2.8". In addition, the survey showed that more than one third (36%) of the representative German population agree that South Africa is a pleasant destination (top-two-box / sum of all "1" and "2" ratings). Another large share of 39% agrees that the travel destination shows a medium level of sympathy (rated "3"). The other 24% of the sympathy ratings for South Africa are allocated to the bottom-two-box group (sum of all "4" and "5" ratings).

As part of the socio-demographic segmentations it could be determined that the sympathy ratings as well are predominantly evenly spread throughout the respective subgroups. Significant differences were only occasionally noted with a clear focus on the segmentation by age groups.

The following chart illustrates how the sympathy ratings for the travel destination South Africa are distributed by age groups.

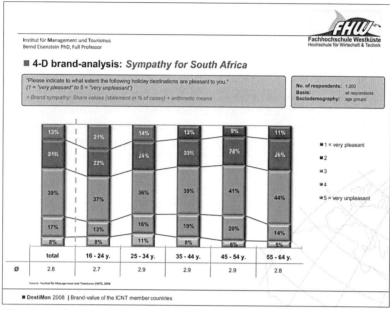

Fig. 2: Evaluation of sympathy for the destination South Africa differentiated by age groups[3]

It is evident that South Africa receives the highest sympathy values among the younger age groups, in particular within the age ranging from 16 to 24 years. Thus only among the group aged 16 to 24 years a value of "2.7" in average were reached. Furthermore in this age group the share of those who considered South Africa to be a pleasant place (top-two-box of 43%) turns out to be significantly above average compared to a value of 36% of all participants questioned.

---

[3] Source: Institut für Management und Tourismus (IMT) (2008).

4.3 Willingness to travel (3rd level)

To determine the willingness to travel the interviewees had to imagine going either on a holiday trip or a short trip and to what extent the destinations at hand would be suitable to them. In this prospective evaluation they had to use a scale of 1 to 5, where "1 = would be very suitable" and "5 = would not be suitable at all".

For the destination South Africa an average value of "3.1" was achieved. Furthermore, it could be determined that at the time of the survey that slightly more than a third of the German population represented (35%) indicates that South Africa, in general, would be suitable as a holiday or short trip destination (top-two-box). Regarding the willingness to travel, another 26% indicates they are indecisive (rating of "3"). In comparison to that, 39% of the interviewees would not spend their holidays or short trip in South Africa (bottom-two-box).

In general, relatively little differences were surveyed again between the respective classes regarding the relevance of South Africa as a future travel destination shown within the socio-demographic segmentations. However, significant differences for criteria such as gender, level of education, and age groups were occasionally determined.

Therefore, with regard to the segmentation by gender, it can be pointed out that for the female ("3.0") interviewees the average willingness to travel is significantly more pronounced than for the male participants ("3.2").

In the case of the classification between the level of education, it could be determined that the share of those who possess a moderate or higher level of education - who would South Africa consider to be a suitable destination - is significantly higher than of those participants who have a lower level of education. The link that the willingness to travel is more pronounced among the part of the population who possesses a higher level of education was also determined for several of the other surveyed destinations, e.g. Argentina, New Zealand, Norway and France.

Additionally, within the group aged 16 to 24 years, South Africa can claim well above-average relevance for a future visit. This is depicted in the following figure.

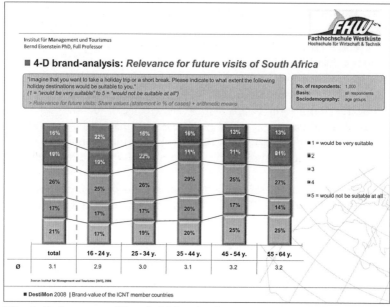

Fig. 3: Relevance of South Africa for future holidays and short trips differentiated by age groups[4]

As a result, the share for the age group 16 to 24 years turned out to be the highest for those who would generally indicate South Africa as a place for a holiday or short trip (top-two-box of 42%) – the same applies for the average willingness to travel ("2.9").

4.4   Personal attachment / visit (4th level)

As already explained, the "four dimensional brand analysis" is completed by the actual visit and/or personal attachment in the respective destination. To determine this retrospective element the participants had to indicate in which of the available travel destinations they had spent their holiday (from one overnight stay) within the last three years.

---

[4] Source: Institut für Management und Tourismus (IMT) (2008).

As a central result of the "visiting behaviour in the past" it can be highlighted that a total of 1.9% of the German population represented in the sample had spent their holiday in South Africa in the past three years.

5. Evaluations compared to further holiday destinations

In the following chapter the survey results for South Africa discussed earlier will be brought into relation with the other destinations surveyed.

5.1 Level of Awareness (1st level)

With an awareness level of 92%, South Africa ranks among the middle range (5th place) in terms of the assisted awareness compared to the other nine ICNT member countries.

The ranking is led by the three European travel destinations surveyed. Besides Norway (94%), these are the traditionally important destinations of the German travel market Spain (97%) and France (97%). They are followed by the long-distance destinations Mexico (93%), South Africa (92%) and New Zealand (92%). Shortly thereafter China (90%), Argentina (90%) and Russia (88%) follow. Macedonia, a relatively new destination that has just recently entered the field of competition, completes the group of travel destinations surveyed with an awareness level of 79%.

5.2 Level of sympathy (2nd level)

Measured against the average rates of the sympathy values, South Africa ranks 6th again within the middle range. The following figure gives an overview of the sympathy values achieved for the travel destinations surveyed.

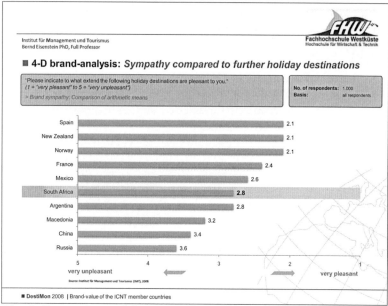

Fig. 4: Comparison of the sympathy values for the travel destinations by means of the average ratings[5]

When comparing the presented ranking of the travel destinations in respect of the assisted awareness, significant changes are occasionally detected: New Zealand ("2.1"), for example, can be found in the group with the highest sympathy values, which still consists of the European destinations Spain ("2.1"), Norway ("2.1") and France ("2.4").

The value of sympathy for Mexico, Argentina and South Africa, however, ranks close to the overall arithmetic average of all travel destinations of "2.71". The gap between South Africa and the destinations

---

[5] Source: Institut für Management und Tourismus (IMT) (2008).

which show the best sympathy values demonstrates as well the (still) existing scope to improve the image on the German source market.

The group of destinations which shows sympathy values below average is led by Macedonia ("3.2") followed by China ("3.4") and Russia ("3.6").

5.3 Willingness to travel (3rd level)

Measured against the average values, the distribution of the considered travel destinations, regarding the willingness to travel of the population represented, is described in a very similar way as shown before in the results relating to sympathy. As the figure below shows, the destinations surveyed, again can be divided into three main groups (having the same group members as it has been the case for the sympathy evaluation).

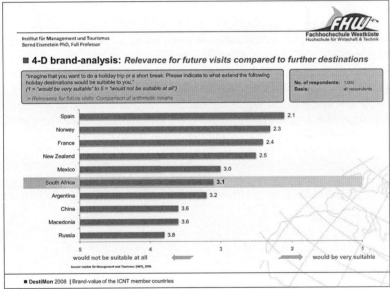

Fig. 5: Comparison of the relevance of the destinations surveyed for future holiday trips and short trips by means of the aver age ratings[6]

---

[6] Source: Institut für Management und Tourismus (IMT) (2008).

The highest relevance for future visits are, as expected, for Spain ("2.1"), which is traditionally one of the most popular travel destinations for Germans (FUR (ed.) 2010, 4). Moreover, destinations such as Norway ("2.3"), France ("2.4") and New Zealand ("2.5") can expect a higher than average willingness to travel.

Of all destinations surveyed the arithmetic average of "2.96" is assigned to Mexico ("3.0"), South Africa ("3.1") and Argentina ("3.2"). With regard to the results for Mexico, it is to be emphasized that the survey was carried out prior to the outbreak of the swine flu. It is assumed that due to the outbreak the willingness for Germans to travel to Mexico declined at least for a short period.

The willingness to travel of the population represented to destinations such as Macedonia ("3.6"), China ("3.6") and Russia ("3.8") is below average.

5.4 Personal attachment / Visit (4th level)

In terms of the personal attachment and/or a visit - i.e. the share of the interviewees, who actually spent their holidays within the last three years in one of the mentioned destinations - relatively huge differences between the destinations surveyed can be found.

The following figure shows the summarized results of the destinations surveyed with regard to the "brand value analysis" levels beginning with the assisted brand awareness up to the "travel behaviour in the past".

	Brand-Awareness (value in % of all cases)	Sympathy value (average value)	Willingness to travel (average value)	Personal attachment / visit (value in % of all cases)
Spain	97%	2.1	2.1	28.2%
France	97%	2.4	2.4	20.8%
Norway	94%	2.1	2.3	3.8%
Mexico	93%	2.6	3.0	2.0%
South Africa	*92%*	*2.8*	*3.1*	*1.9%*
New Zealand	92%	2.1	2.5	1.3%
China	90%	3.4	3.6	1.0%
Argentina	90%	2.8	3.2	0.4%
Russia	88%	3.6	3.8	2.5%
Macedonia	79%	3.2	3.6	0.6%
None of the named destinations	1.5%	-	-	57.5%
Number of all respondents: 1,000 *Basis:* all respondents				

Fig. 6: Results of the customer-oriented brand value assessment of the German source market for all destinations surveyed[7]

The two travel destinations which show by far the strongest personal attachment are Spain (28.2%) and France (20.8%). While Norway follows with a share of 3.8% all other destinations show values within a range of 2.5% (Russia) and 0.4% (Argentina). South Africa can be found within that range as well (1.9%). Furthermore, more than a half (57.5%) of the population group represented in the sample spent their holidays within the last three years in none of the destinations mentioned.

---

[7] Source: Institut für Management und Tourismus (IMT) (2008).

6. Conclusion

To gain insights in the attitude of the represented German population towards South Africa as a tourist destination, to what extent they find the location attractive, and whether they would spend their holiday or short trip in that destination, the "brand value analysis"-model was specifically applied for the research objective of the special study shown here.

As a result, South Africa can already refer to a high assisted awareness level of 92% as a travel destination. In addition, it could be determined that 36% of the population represented thinks of South Africa as a pleasant destination (top-two-box), plus slightly more than one third of the Germans are willing to spend their holidays in South Africa (top-two-box).

On the basis of the customer-oriented brand value assessment, it can be concluded that the Germans, in general, show a positive attitude towards South Africa as a travel destination. Nonetheless, compared to the other ICNT countries, South Africa is consistently found within the middle range. This gives reason to further derive (significant) scope to improve the customer-oriented brand strength on the German source market.

Furthermore, socio-demographic segmentations were carried out in order to detect additional market potentials by applying the "brand value analysis" levels for South Africa under the aspects of gender, age, level of education and heritage (classified by ACNielsen). In general, relatively little differences between each category could be determined here. In this context, however, it should be emphasized that both the sympathy ratings and the willingness to travel between those aged 16 to 24 years are pronounced (significantly) above average. For this age group this could represent one segment of South Africa which needs to be pinpointed directly on the German source market.

For a final overall classification of the results presented, it is to be pointed out that the analyzed contributory factors of brand awareness (cognitive), brand sympathy (affective) and willingness to travel (conative) play an important role in the travel decision. But if the research objective should aim for a comprehensive evaluation of the opportunities for South Africa to participate successfully in the market, a wide range of contributory key factors would be taken into account additionally (cp. Ritchie / Crouch 2005, 60sqq.). This, for instance, is the development of travel behaviour of Germans, current tourism trends, development trends of competitive environments, accessibility of the destination South Africa and the travel costs involved as well as the current stage of development of the destination with regard to the destination life cycle.

7. Perspective

The surveys conducted on a quarterly basis (survey waves) using the IMT's Destination Monitor would provide the opportunity to repeat the customer-oriented brand value assessment for the ICNT countries. By carrying out evaluations periodically, the success for instance of marketing measures introduced could be highlighted. Currently, a particular research interest for the travel destination South Africa would be to what extent the FIFA World Cup in the summer of 2010 will influence the perception of the destination for the source market Germany in the short-, medium-, and long-term.

Moreover, there would also be options for a continual expansion to further increase the validity of the study results for the ICNT member countries in case of a repetition. That way, basic brand characteristics like "uniqueness", "needs orientation", "authenticity", "familiarity", "quality" and "affordability" could be added to the "brand value analysis" model. Additionally, spontaneous associations of the represented German population with the respective travel destination could be surveyed, so that more qualified ratings for the ICNT member countries in the German source market are determined.

References

Eisenstein, Bernd / Müller, Sylvia / Heubeck, Melanie (ed.) (2009): *Destination Brand 09. Markenstärke für deutsche Reiseziele.* Heide/Holstein.

FUR Forschungsgemeinschaft Urlaub und Reisen e. V. (ed.) (2010): *Die 40. Reiseanalyse RA 2010. Erste Ergebnisse ITB 2010.* 25.04.2010.
http://www.fur.de/fileadmin/user_upload/RA_Zentrale_Ergebnisse/FUR_Re iseanalyse_RA2010_Erste_Ergebnisse.pdf.

Gruner + Jahr AG & Co KG (ed.) (2008): *STERN MarkenProfile 12 – Einführung.* 25.04.2010.
http://www.gujmedia.de/_components/markenprofile/mapro12/download/d atein/MaPro12-Einfuehrung.pdf.

Gruner + Jahr AG & Co KG (ed.) (2001): *STERN MarkenProfile 9 – Banken inkl. Direktbanken und Online-Broker.* 25.04.2010.
http://www.gujmedia.de/_components/markenprofile/pdf_download/MaPro 9_Banken.pdf.

Ramme, Iris (2000): *Marketing: Einführung mit Fallbeispielen, Aufgaben und Lösungen.* 1. edition. Stuttgart.

Ritchie, J.R. Brent / Crouch, Geoffrey I. (2005): *The competitive destination: a sustainable tourism perspective.* 2. edition. Wellingford.

The Impact of the Internet on Silver Surfers' Leisure Travel Information Search

Alice Gräupl

1. Introduction

Older people do not think they are old. That is the first thing they will tell you about themselves. They see themselves as a group that has still a lot to live for after the children have moved out. They enjoy their new found freedom amongst other things by travelling the globe. (Muller and O'Cass, 2001). Literature in general has so far underestimated the power of the "grey market" and only few studies have concentrated on them in regards to Internet usage (Muller and O'Cass, 2001; Trocchia and Janda, 2000; Eastman and Iyer, 2004; etc.), which is why it was chosen for this research.

The online information search is an important aspect of the tourism decision-making process and has been looked at by researchers since the late nineties (Jang, 2004), however, few concentrate on a pure search that relies on the individual rather than technology. Within the context of this study, the (online) information search is seen as a knowledge building experience based process that does not necessarily lead to an immediate purchase decision. Experience and knowledge play such an important role that during the early stages of the study, the author started out by looking at cultural and behavioural theories rather than technological inventions and systems that claim to make online information searching and decision-making easier for travellers e.g. recommender systems etc. This study builds on the belief that anybody can use Information & Communications Technologies to support the experience based, knowledge building information search process.

2.   Theoretical background

2.1   Online information search

The online information search has received growing interest from researchers especially in the tourism area during the last years. Sheldon (1993a) has once called information the life-blood of the tourism industry which can be argued is the main reason of the significance of the information search within the travel decision-making process. Information technology has, through its rapid development especially in the tourism industry, significantly influenced information search behaviour in travel and tourism decision-making (Jang, 2004). It is important to state that within the context of this study, the (online) information search is seen as a knowledge building, experience based process rather than a goal orientated one. Unlike convenience shopping goods, decisions to purchase travel products/services are not made immediately once the information search has ended. It is a long process that forces the person doing the research to deliberate and consider all the possible options available. Since travelling decisions are of such importance for the individual, the decision is not made hastily.

There are distinct differences between off- and online information search. Generally speaking, "online information search usually refers to information search activity through the Internet" (Jang, 2004, p. 43). A distinct advantage of an online information search is that it allows prospective travellers to search and compare at the same time. The nature of the tourism "product" has a big influence since the quality of the "product" is not certain until it is experienced, therefore a more in-depth information search can reassure the prospective traveller in their decision. (Jang, 2004) This is one of many reasons why the tourism industry has been greatly affected by the introduction of the Internet (Weber and Roehl, 1999).

The Internet offers a wide range of information and resources to travellers (Susskind et al, 2003), but it also offers suppliers the possibility of getting to know their prospective consumers better (using search and purchase records). Information intermediaries can help provide suppliers with profiles of travellers and their selection of products that they bought based on their needs (Palmer and McCole, 2000).

The online information search offers both benefits to travellers and marketers as well as concerns and opportunities. One of the biggest benefits is that websites are cost efficient for suppliers – a website is "open" 24/7 and allows the consumer instant access to the information needed. It can also be used as a real-time communication tool, especially when considering new tools like live chats, etc. Various authors (e.g. Hoffman and Novak, 1997; Wang et al, 2002) have pointed out the primary advantages or online search to travellers. They are relative low cost, customised information, ease of product comparisons, interactivity, virtual community formation and 24 hour accessibility [...]. According to Bellman et al (1999) online purchasers believe that the online search on the Internet has improved the overall productivity of their purchase process. From a suppliers' point of view, they can enhance the efficiency of their distribution, be it information, products or services due to cost-effectiveness and immediate interactivity (Connolly et al, 1998). Another benefit that is particularly relevant to the tourism industry is, that the Internet freely reaches anywhere in the world (as long as you have access to it), which means that the potential market has no national or international boundary (Jang, 2004). Due to "the distinctive high-price, high-involvement, and well-differentiated characteristics of the travel products and services", online marketing seems to be a well-suited approach for the tourism industry (Bonn et al, 1998). There seems to be an agreement amongst authors that the Internet provides advantages like global accessibility, convenience in updating, real-time information service, interactive communications features and unique customisation capabilities (Bender, 1997) as well as a general opinion that using the Internet can enable destinations to improve their competitiveness by increasing their visibility, reducing advertising costs, and assist local cooperation (Buhalis, 2000). It is also important to look at concerns and opportunities. Machlis (1997) pointed out that people visit travel websites mainly for information purposes and less than 5 percent actually buy travel or tourism products online. These figures have not changed much; a recent comScore study for Google has shown the major importance online searching in influencing offline buying on consumers' travel related purchases (comScore, 2006). Possible reasons for this behaviour are technical difficulties, credit card security, no assessment of product quality, and privacy issues (Szymanski and Hise, 2000; Weber and Roehl, 1999). It is of major importance that tourism marketers consider these concerns when building/designing a website and developing online marketing programmes (Jang, 2004). Jang (2004) furthermore points out that his research has shown that various research studies have claimed that website features are a significant variable that relates online information search to actual purchase action (Chu, 2001; Metha and Shah, 2001).

In order for a website to be competitive, it has been argued that providers should supply specified information e.g. product perceptions, shopping experience, customer service and customer risks (Jarvenpaa and Todd, 1997). The aspect of what information should be offered is an extremely important factor in the tourism industry due to the nature of the product. Here are some examples of what kind of information should be provided; activities in the destination, destination information, sightseeing, maps, "insider tips", accommodation, shopping, festival and events, and also reservations (Tierney, 2000).

2.2   The forgotten segment – the "grey market"

Not surprisingly most research has shown that the "average" online information user is young, male, well educated and has a well paid job (Bonn et al 1999; Fram and Grady, 1995; Pitkow and Kehoe, 1996). Morrison et al (2001) support these findings by stating that the 26-34 years old age group and people with higher education were more likely buy travel online as opposed to offline. Additionally, Weber and Roehl (1999) also support this argument, stating that those who search for (and purchase) travel related products online are more likely to be young, to have higher incomes, to be employed in management jobs, and to have more online experience.

Although true to a certain extent, these findings can be very misleading to both researchers and information providers. Obviously, the younger age groups present a large proportion of the online market; however, they are by far not the only group that will use the Internet. The older age groups might have been slower to "get on board" but the numbers of "silver surfers" are growing.

The overall population of the UK (in which this study is based) is 58.7 million people of whom 18.4 percent – 10.8 million people – were over the pensionable age; this number is projected to increase to 11.2 million in 2006 and to 11.9 million in 2011. In 2002 about 6 million people between the age of 50 and state pension age were still in employment – for men between 50 and 64 years this equals to an employment rate of 70 percent, for women between 50 and 59 years it is 65.5 percent.

Most interesting is that in 2000, 25 percent of households with 2 adults aged 60 or over and 7 percent of single person households aged

60 or over owned a computer. Furthermore in July 2002, 44 percent of people aged 55 to 64, and 14 percent of people aged 65 and over had used the Internet.[1]

Long ignored and characterised as a politically and socially insignificant homogenous group, marketers have finally realised the negligible spending power of this market segment. Older consumers, the grey market, have partly been misrepresented in both the media and society and been shown as being incapable of many everyday occurrences. (Gunter, 1998)

With their children having left home and their loans paid off, empty nesters in modern western societies may have plenty of disposable income, particularly before retirement.

2.3 Lifestage changes

Due to the particular make up of each lifestage there exist very distinct behavioural patterns. The various choices that members in each lifestage make are much to do with their individual structures as it is to do with the market factors by which they are overseen. However, as consumers progress from one lifestage into another the question must be asked how much of the market is predisposed by the requirements of these consumers and how much is dependent on the holiday packages that are created for them by leading companies in the sector. There is a trend, a tendency towards sophisticated of personalised holidays, this them means that companies have acknowledged a certain degree of demand push by consumers who are becoming more knowledgeable. Technologies such as the Internet have meant that consumers now have fast access to information, which raises their anticipations in terms of the holidays that they are either able to secure via direct booking or via packages that they then request from travel agents. (Mintel, 2000)

Empty nester and post families: having time, money and freedom from responsibilities of looking after children, these lifestages tend to go on several holidays a year (often mixing short breaks in the UK and/or Europe with long-haul holidays). Because of their higher disposable income, both of these lifestages are an important segment for the industry. (Mintel, 2000)

Consumers are becoming increasingly aware of the holiday options available to them. The reason for this development is due to the

---

[1] All information was provided by National statistics (2002).

"invasion" of specific information technologies e.g. the Internet, etc. Thus, both leading tour operators and travel agents have reacted by developing their websites to provide for those who require information on destinations, flights and accommodation.

The accessibility of these websites and increased consumer sophistication has fuelled the increase in consumers booking their holidays independently or direct with tour operators and airlines.

Consumer research illustrates that one of the key driving forces for the industry in the next few years will continue to be the different requirements of the main lifestage groups. More and more consumers have access to better information and as consumers become more familiar with using some of the new technologies such as e.g. the Internet; their holiday requirements will continue to be more sophisticated. For the industry this means that they need to continuously invest in e-commerce and use a combination of media by which to communicate and target their consumers.

Eastman and Iyer (2004) support the argument that although the Internet has grown during the last years, there is a distinctive lack of research in the area of Internet usage in the older market segments. The rapid growth of this particular segment as well as the potential held by the Internet are both subjects worth of consideration. Studies in the USA have shown that elderly consumers have positive intentions towards using the Internet and their willingness of learning how to use it. Education and income levels have both had a favourable impact on Internet usage, too. (Eastman and Iyer, 2004).

O'Leary (2000) has argued that the Web is becoming more of a mass medium and "seniors are now one of the fastest growing groups of new Web users" (O'Leary, 2000, p. 80). This quote states the need for more consideration of the senior citizens as a viable possible market. Marketers need to realise that they are actually losing a feasible segment that could me more profits in the long run. Apart from the argument of an ageing population (especially with baby boomers reaching the age of 65 from 2011 onwards) and therefore the sheer number of older people, it is also important not to forget that seniors usually have more disposable income and buying power than other market segments (Eastman and Iyer, 2004). Polyak (2000) argued that seniors have approximately twice the discretionary income. That would make them particularly interesting for the tourism industry especially when adding that they also have more free time (particularly when they are already retired). Trocchia and Janda have put it best when saying that "older consumers comprise a growing but under-represented segment of Internet users" (2000: 605). Schofield (1999) called senior citizens the fastest growing groups on the Internet because they have the time to be active and pursue their interests due to better healthcare and medical advances. Many of today's seniors want an active retirement learning new skills (Gardyn, 2000).

The increasing technological society has to address the barriers and means necessary to allow older individuals to join the information age. It is not only important to realise the economic benefit that can arise from targeting older consumers but also the potential improvement in the quality of their life which may be gained through online communication by a person who may otherwise not be able to (McMellon and Schiffman, 2000). This takes the argument even further as this thesis concentrates on the proportion of the grey market that is still able to travel and enjoy their lives by being active and being able to physically visiting places.

It is a common misconception that older people are not interested in technological advances. It is valid to say, that not all of them have or will embrace Information Technology but it is very rare that something actually works for everyone. Zeithaml and Gilly (1987) have looked at how senior have adopted past technological advances and found that e.g. retail technologies were accepted when a clear advantage is offered and communicated. The more affluent and exposed to print media seem to be the ones most open to try new technologies. So, even pre-Internet research indicates that older people will use new technologies as long as there is a clear benefit. The perceived techno-phobia of older people has decreased during the last years, and more seniors have become PC users at home. Ownership alone has increased from 29 to 40 percent between 1995 and 1998 in the USA (Portland State University, 2000). Avalos (1998) stated that 70 percent of US citizens ages 55 and above have Internet access at home.

The "grey market" is both a growing and under-represented segment of Internet users. In comparison to younger users, these people possess more time and income, which makes them a very important sector of the market. This presents a significant opportunity for the providers of Internet related products and services. Trocchia & Janda (2000) conducted interviews with six Internet users and six non-users (six men and six women between 57 and 87 years old) in order to better understand the attitudes and motivations of the "grey market". Their research came up with six leading themes that will show similarity with the author's own research: reference group affiliation, technology schema, resistance to change, nature of social relations, perception of reality, and physical dexterity.

3. Methodology

Deeply rooted in a positivist paradigm, consumer behaviour research usually lends itself to a deductive approach (Solomon et al, 1999). Remaining aware of the existing theory, this research takes a more inductive approach testing out new research methods. According to Finn et al (2000) a positivist paradigm strives for explanation, prediction and control as well as processes for explaining human behaviour. This study aims to identify and examine experiences and processes of "grey" travel information search without an immediate purchase intention within a post-positivist framework.

The design of the study chosen is emergent, inductive (Silverman, 2001) to the issues of information search needs amongst the "grey market". Remaining acquainted with the existing theory of consumer behaviour, however testing question styles and approaches to targeting and selection of participants.

Multiple methods approaches have become quite common in research (Veal, 1997). The way in which methods can be combined varies; combining methods is not constricted to methods within one approach i.e. one can also "triangulate" methods from both qualitative and quantitative approaches (Silverman, 2001). This study takes a triangulated approach, combing both quantitative (questionnaires) and qualitative (interviews) methods. The interviews helped inform the questions used for the questionnaire. While the sample of interviewees was rather small (6 participants), the responses received from the questionnaire were considerably larger (517 valid answers).

The relevant sample population for the research consists first of all of individuals as it is the individuals' behaviour and experiences that the investigation aims to identify. The only restrictions to the sample are age – the sample consists of people over 50 years of age – and that the person must be an active Internet user and geographic location. The age cap of 50 years was determined by both statistics and previous research experience. It was concluded that people from the age of 50 years onwards will help provide the study with a good mix of both still working as well as retired people. There are no restrictions concerning gender, occupation or geographic location within the UK.

This study relied on a combination of sampling methods. The author started out with a convenience sample which involves either asking for volunteers or a set of people who just happen to be available (Black, 1999) hence there is no way of ensuring that the sample is representative of the population. In this particular case, the researcher started out with known "silver surfers" in the realm of her acquaintances as well as by contacting websites that target "silver surfers". People were asked if they would be willing to participate in study about online behaviour in the "grey market". Once the convenience sample was put into place, it morphed into a snowball sample. A snowball sample happens when people with desired.

The rationale behind choosing a combination of the above mentioned samples is that a random sample within the chosen age group would consist of too many non-Internet users. Although Internet usage is increasing within the "grey" market segment the majority of over 50-year-old persons is still not connected to the Internet (Statistics Canada, 2003). As the research focuses on the Internet users within this age group, so-called "silver surfers", it would not be reasonable to build this research on a random sample. Furthermore, the combination of samples helped to reach more people since all respondents are asked to pass on the questionnaire to friends and family.

Concerning distribution, the questionnaire was distributed via e-mail, asking several websites catering for "silver surfers" to send out the survey in their newsletters. Some websites were eager to cooperate, however, for confidentiality reasons, the researcher was asked not to mention how many responses were received from which specific websites. The exact sample size could not be determined before hand due to snowball sampling, however, the researcher was aiming for around 500 valid responses and in the end 517 valid ones were received.

4. Discussion and results

The following discussion looks at selected results from both the qualitative and quantitative data collected.

4.1 General Internet usage and behaviour

To say that the interest and online behaviour is diverse would be an understatement. The respondents demonstrate a deep understanding of online activities. Overall, length of Internet usage is not related to the age of the respondents. Most people have been using the Internet for 4-

6 years; however a higher number of people have been using the Internet for longer than 6 or less than 4 years. That would indicate that most respondents started using the Internet between 1998 and 2000 or earlier.

It is important to make a distinction between respondents who are already retired and those who still in the active workforce. Interestingly, even half of those who are retired stated that they started using the Internet for work purposes (most likely back in the days when they were not yet retired). Out of those still working, those that started using it for work purposes are slightly in the lead. Interest in new technologies and a desire to keep up to date with new gadgets can certainly be considered an important influence. Even if more respondents started the Internet for work purposes, the difference between the two numbers is minimal (51 answers) so a definite trend cannot be established.

When we look back to length of Internet usage, we saw that most respondents started using the Internet 4-6 years ago. The research has shown that that most of them taught themselves, followed by taking a computer course. Overall most respondents indicated that they have learnt by doing, about a fifth of the respondents took advantage of computer courses and almost even numbers of respondents asked for help from their colleagues or families. When comparing that to the fact that most participants started using the Internet at work, it would seem unusual that the employer did not provide employees with a starter course. It is also acknowledged that since technologies change constantly, the learning process is in fact an on-going one.

4.2   Information search behaviour

One of the most important aspects when it comes to online information search is the question whether or not respondents find the information they need. The responses were balanced with half of the interviewees being quite confident and stating they would find anything on the Internet if they set their mind to it and the other half admitting that it looks a lot easier than it actually is.

"If I need information, I will not stop looking for it till I have found it. I just have to make sure that I use the correct keywords in the search engine."

"Again, I have to say that I thought the Internet would be easier to use. The lack of index is still a problem for me. I know how to use search engines but somehow it's not the same."

Everybody maintained that although they think the Internet is a good information source, they always back up their information search with other information sources e.g. travel guide books and brochures.

"Even though I know that I can find all the information on the Internet, I will still buy a [Lonely Planet] guide book. Not only so that I can take it on holiday but also because it helps to back up my online information searches."

One interviewee mentioned that for him the search on the Internet is like a process of knowledge build-up. You learn where to go to find information and experience [knowledge build-up] teaches you to comprehend which ones [websites, search engines, etc.] to use. This blends in with the argument the author has built up in the literature section. The information search is indeed not just a means to an end in one particular case but what you experience will be remembered for future purposes.

The reasons why people stated that they could not find what they look for were impatience with search engines and also that it obviously depends on the topic that you are researching.

"Even though I have plenty of leisure time I don't want to sit in front of the computers for hours. If I can find it quickly I will look at it, if not I will go somewhere else."

One interviewee stated that she could not always find what she is looking for, however referred to her research for work rather than her travel related searches.

The questionnaire respondents of this study have shown that to a great extent they always find what they are looking for. Twenty-five percent stated that they only find parts of the information or it takes them longer to search (13 percent), however, they do tend to find what they want – interestingly these issues seem more prominent in the younger age groups. The numbers of people who do not find what they are looking for are very low … and can surely be improved by some effort from the providers. It is also important to remember that this question was not asked in relation to tourism but in a general "Can you find information on the Internet?" way.

The actual percentage of people claiming they cannot find any information online is 3 percent. In a sample of 517 people over the age of 50, the author expected a higher percentage than the result.

The questionnaire respondents that answered no to the previous question about whether or not they find the information they are looking for were asked to answer an additional question concerning what they consider to be the main problem with the Internet. When looking at these reasons, it can be said that most of them feel that there is just too much information available (62 percent). Nineteen percent think the Internet is not structured enough and the same percentage thinks that search engines are not specific enough. It is also interesting to see that all respondents who had problems finding information are male.

4.3   Information searched for by the "grey market"

One of the most important issues of this research study is what kind of tourism related information "silver surfers" search for. The graph below outlines the various choices the respondents had and how many within each age group ticked a certain box. Because this question allowed respondents to answer multiple times, it is not feasible to provide a graph that shows percentages.

	Age					Total
	50-54 years	55-59 years	60-64 years	65-74 years	75 years +	
Flights	200	150	52	49	16	467
Accommodation info	184	116	52	66	16	434
Price	183	133	35	33	16	400
Other transport	184	116	35	17	16	368
Climate, weather	151	118	34	33	16	352
Country entry requirements	149	126	54	3	18	350
Destinations, visitor attractions	167	118	34	0	16	335
Independent travellers	67	68	34	16	0	185
Tour operators	67	68	17	16	0	168
Package holidays	84	51	17	0	0	152
Special interest tourism	67	51	17	0	0	135
Information on animal welfare	0	17	0	0	0	17

Table 4.1: Information search for by the "grey market"

The table above shows the respondents' answers to the question what tourism related topics they researched on the Internet.

Most respondents have searched for information on flights, followed by accommodation information and price. When looking at the most researched topics in the various age groups, the findings are as follows:

The most researched topic in any age group was flights in the 50-54 years segment; in the 55-59 years segment it was also flights; in the 60-64 years segment it was country entry requirements; in the 65-74 years segment it was accommodation information; in the 75 years or older segment it was country entry requirements.

One of the surprising results is that destination information is only ranked 7th among 12 subjects. More than a fifth of all respondents have stated in a later question that they have used additional sources during their information search so an assumption can be made that destination information is one of the subjects (as it is also one of the first decisions made according to the results of this study) where respondents rely on more traditional data sources. A guess would be that most people, just like the author, rely on well known guidebooks and only check for up to date information (like e.g. museum opening hours and entrance fees) online. These results are also slightly contradictory to interview findings where interviewees stated that one of their main topics searched for on the Internet is destination information.

Additionally, specific travel information like e.g. package holidays etc. does not seem to be relevant for this market segment. The least researched topic was by far Information on animal welfare, followed by special interest tourism and package holidays. It has to be acknowledged that information on animal welfare is definitely a very specialised topic that is only relevant to a certain sub group of people (obviously those who own pets and have to leave them during their holidays), however, the number on special interest tourism could have been higher. In particular when thinking that people are getting more sophisticated and selective when it comes to deciding on a holiday, one could have assumed that highly specialised information would be high on their list, but then again the assumption can be made that respondents used different forms of information sources for the acquirement of this data.

The fact that price is ranked 2nd can lead to the assumption that the Internet is still seen as a cheap alternative as well as a tool to compare prices between competitors anonymously, efficiently and fast.

Finally, the reason why flights is ranked as the most searched for topic can be traced back to the emergence of low cost airlines, which are mainly booked online (most are bookable via the phone but offer an additional discount when booked online). These airlines are of great importance for any traveller planning their own holidays as they might prove to be the cheapest means of transportation especially for domestic or European short breaks and/or holidays.

During the interviews, respondents were asked regarding using the Internet for leisure holidays. Five out of six interviewees state that they book regularly on the Internet, which is a small contradiction to one of the hypotheses that implied that the Internet is still mainly used as an information source rather than a booking tool. However, such a small sample of people is not really representative of the general activities of the "grey market". Nevertheless it is interesting to see that the majority of the interviewees do book online and not only for rail tickets and car hire but also for plane tickets (and not only for low-cost airlines, although those were emphasised because as one interviewee stated "you have no choice") and even for independently arranged holidays.

"It is just so convenient. I can do it at home whenever I want. No need to go to the travel agency or call anyone. Just sit down, click and book."

"I just prefer to arrange my own holidays. I can never really find the perfect package holiday so it's much easier to just pick and choose and then book it right away."

Generally, the other activities are typical information search for leisure and holiday related matters, e.g. checking on flight times, airport parking and particularly destination information, which was mentioned by the majority.

"I can check flight times so much easier online. I can try out different days and nobody is annoyed [like a travel agent] if I want to check 5 different days. Plus I don't feel bad for taking up somebody else's time."

Destination information is one of the main topics that were researched on the Internet, either before deciding on a holiday or to back up a decision as well as after the decision was made in order to gain a better knowledge of the destination chosen.

"The reason why I used the Internet to look up destination information is simple. I can find a lot of information for free and that's important when I haven't decided yet where to go. I can always buy a [Lonely Planet] travel guide book once I've made a specific decision."

In general, the topics researched are basic issues that would otherwise have been addressed with either the travel agent or by buying a travel guide or asking friends for experience.

4.4   Information needs of the "grey market"

One of the aspects that became apparent during the secondary research and then again during the earlier pilot study (please see Graeupl and McCabe, 2002) was that it seemed the Internet was mainly aimed at the younger online population. Respondents were simply asked to rank how much they agree with the statement that 'the Internet is too youth orientated' on a 5 stage Likert scale.

		Age					Total
		50-54 years	55-59 years	60-64 years	65-74 years	75 years or older	
Internet too youth orientated?	Strongly agree	0	0	0	0	0	0
	Agree	33	33	0	16	0	82
	Neutral	34	0	0	16	16	66
	Disagree	99	59	20	3	2	183
	Strongly disagree	51	66	35	34	0	186
Total		217	158	55	69	18	517

Table 4.2: Internet too youth orientated?

The outcome of this question contradicts the working hypotheses that the Internet does not provide the information that is required by this particular market segment.

Interviewees and questionnaire respondents stated that they do think the Internet caters for their age groups. Only 82 out of a possible 517 respondents (16 percent) agree with the statement that the information provided on the Internet is too youth orientated. The respondents stated that there is information for all age groups out there; you just have to find it. Even more people stated that they strongly disagree (36 percent) than "just" disagree (35 percent).

Admittedly, these results were unexpected as the author assumed that the general consensus in the "grey market" would be that the information provided on the Internet is not directly aimed at them.

However, an assumption can be made that there has to be made an important distinction between information that is directly aimed at the "grey market" – e.g. special senior traveller websites or online communities for older people – and information that is simply not aimed at the youth market in particular – e.g. general information that can either be travel related or not. The author acknowledges that these results are not representative of the entire "grey market" population; however, there is a clear trend within this group that they do not feel neglected by the online information providers.

Generally, when referring to specific information needs of an older i.e. 50+ person, the interviewees agreed that the information provided does meet their needs. A few exceptions were specific personal preferences e.g. pictures that can be viewed 360° (e.g. for hotel websites). Basically, they are all saying that there is information out there for everyone and that you just need the skills to find it. The more experience you have, the better you get at finding what you really need (again knowledge build-up).

"It took me some time but now I really think that I can find all the information I need online."

Overall they think that the information is not too youth orientated and that they usually look for information at different places that the younger generations.

"I can see why people think the Internet is too youth orientated but the truth is that there is information on there for everyone. It might take some time till you find it but there are even sites that are especially made for older people. They also post links so you know where you have to go to find the specific things you want or need."

One interviewee stated that there are special sites for older people and that one should make use of these sites and generally be more selective. Another one stated that sometimes concerning travel related sites, the information cannot be found there but on other sites. Again, no matter how good the information is, it is usually backed up by other information sources. The issue of the Internet being to youth orientated links us to the next question.

When asked whether they think people of different age groups need specific information, all but one agreed that they do. They all concur that the younger generations are more interested in social aspects of the Internet and information about social events, too. It was also stated that they believe that younger people spend a considerable amount of time on the Internet whereas they like to finish up their searches etc. as quickly as possible and sometimes even get tired of/from looking at the computer screen.

"I don't want to spend all day looking for information on the Internet. I mainly use it when I know what I need, look it up and shut it down again."

There are certainly specific issues that seem to be more interesting to older generations e.g. health issues and probably more culture and historical information. Again, it is mentioned that experience plays an important part regarding knowledge build-up and knowing where to find the information that you are looking for. A problem that was also mentioned is that sometimes the specific information that someone requires is out of date and therefore useless.

"Once I looked up restaurant opening hours on the Internet and when we arrived at the location, they had changed their designated non trading day of the week and haven't updated it on their website so we had to go and find another place to eat. [And obviously didn't go back at another time either.]"

So, if different age groups require different information, the providers should make sure that the particular information required is always up to date.

Not surprisingly, most respondents use additional information sources to back up their online information search either always (45 percent) or often (36 percent). Only 19 percent claim that they never back up the information found online. The majority not using any additional information sources are to be found in the younger age groups. As expected, travel guidebooks are a significant source of information for respondents of all age groups (62 percent), by far beating off the competition; brochures (45 percent) came in 2nd place. Newspapers and magazines (26 percent) again, seem to be more used by the younger age groups and the same goes for the TV (23 percent) as an information source.

Overall, the results were as expected with the travel guidebooks in a clear lead. This is a trend that has become apparent throughout all parts of the data collection. Guidebooks are definitely the most important offline information source for senior travellers.

This leads us to an important factor – how much is the Internet trusted by respondents of this questionnaire?

Overall, it can be said that the respondents of this questionnaire do generally trust the travel related information they find and/or have found on the Internet as 48 percent stated that their trust is either complete or to a certain extent. However, a high number of respondents – 39 percent – state that the decision whether or not they trust travel related information depends on the provider of such information; this became very apparent during the interviews when respondents made it very clear that there is no such thing as blind trust for them. The remaining 13 percent are rather hesitant and stated that they are very cautious when it comes to trusting online information. The fact that more of the younger respondents stated that they are very cautious of the information provided is rather surprising when comparing to previous results that they are the ones who use less additional information sources. These results are rather contradictory. The author expected the results to reflect that the older age groups are more suspicious of the information made available.

5.   Conclusion, limitations and future research
Generally, the results of this study have shown that the "grey market" is not as different from other market segments as expected. The "silver surfers" do have certain requirements for information to be more detailed and up to date as well as they look at different types of information than younger age groups. The older market segment is definitely a very viable one for the tourism industry and it is important that it is not being neglected by the industry. An increased awareness is necessary so that the "grey market" can live up to its potential.

There are several limitations to this study that can be addressed by further research possibilities. Sampling is the most important limitation of this research. First of all, the respondents were limited to a specific geographic location, the United Kingdom. Further research can look at different countries or maybe even continents and explore behaviour of the "grey market" there. Another aspect is that of trying out a new method of data collection – e-surveying (Litvin and Kar, 2001). Although it added on a unique aspect of research, the method used was definitely not easy to implement. If distribution was improved a bigger group of "silver surfers" can be reached in the future.

References

Avalos, G. (1998, October 26). Never too old to surf, *Daily Oregonian.*

Bellman, S., Lohse, G., & Johnson, E.J. (1999). Predictors of online buying behavior. *Communications of the ACM, 42*(12), 32-38.

Bender, D.E. (1997). Using the web to market the hospitality, travel and tourism product or services. *HSMAI Marketing Review, 14*(3), 33-37.

Black, T.R. (1999) Doing Quantitative Research in the Social Science: *An integrated approach to research design, measurement and statistics.* London: Sage.

Bonn, M.A., Furr, H.L., & Susskind, A.M. (1998). Using the Internet as a pleasure travel planning tool: An examination of the sociodemographic and behavioural characteristics among Internet users and nonusers. *Journal of Hospitality and Tourism Research, 22*(3), 303-317.

Bonn, M.A., Furr, H.L., & Susskind, A.M. (1999). Predicting a behavioural profile for pleasure travellers on the basis of Internet use segmentation. *Journal of Travel Research, 37*(4), 333-340.

Buhalis, D. (2000). Marketing the competitive destination of the future. *Tourism Management, 21*(1), 97-116.

Chu, R. (2001). What online Hong Kong travellers look for on airline/travel websites? *International Journal of Hospitality Management, 19*(2), 191-203.

comScore (2006) Retrieved September 2006 from http://www.comscore.com.

Eastman, J.K., & Iyer, R. (2004). The elderly's uses and attitudes towards the Internet. *Journal of Consumer Marketing, 21*(3), 208-220.

Finn, M., Elliott-White, M., & Walton, M. (2000). *Tourism & Leisure Research Methods: Data collection, analysis and interpretation.* Harlow: Pearson Longman.

Fram, E.H., & Grady, D.B. (1995). Internet buyers: Will the surfers become buyers? *Direct Marketing, 58*(6), 63-65.

Gardyn, R. (2000). Retirement redefined, American Demographics, November. Retrieved June 2001 from http://www.demographics.com/publications.

Gunter, B. (1998). *Understanding the older consumer: the grey market.* London: Routledge.

Hoffman, D.L., & Novak, T.P. (1997). A new marketing paradigm for electronic commerce. *The Information Society, 13*, 43-54.

Jang, S. (2004). The past, present, and future research of online information search. *Journal of Travel & Tourism Marketing, 17*(2/3), 41-47.

Jarvenpaa, S.L., & Todd, P.A. (1997). Consumer reactions to electronic shopping on the World Wide Web. *International Journal of Electronic Commerce, 1*(2), 59-88.

Machlis, S. (1997). Profits eludes travel sites. *Comuputerworld, 32*, 53-54.

Metha, K.T., & Shah, V. (2001). E-commerce: The next global frontier for small business. *The Journal of Applied Business Research, 17*(1), 87-94.

Mintel International Group Limited (2000, September). Holidays by Lifestage.

Morrison, A.M., Su, J., O'Leary, J.T., & Cai, L. (2001). Predicting usage of the Internet for travel booking: An exploratory study. *Information Technology and Tourism, 4*(1), 15-30.

Muller, T.E., & O'Cass, A. (2001). Targeting the young at heart: Seeing senior vacationers the way they see themselves. *Journal of Vacation Marketing, 7*(4), 285-301.

National statistics (2002). Retrieved July 2004 from http://www.statistics.co.uk.

O'Leary, M. (2000). Web goes mainstream from everybody. *Online, 24*(6), 80-82.

Palmer, A., & McCole, P. (2000). The role of electronic commerce in creating virtual tourism destination marketing organisations. *International Journal of Contemporary Hospitality Management, 12*(3), 198-204.

Pitkow, J.E., & Kehoe, C.M. (1996). Emerging trends in the WWW user population. *Communications of the ACM, 39*(6), 106-108.

Polyak, I. (2000). The center of attention, *American Demographics, 22*(11), 30-32.

Portland State University (2000). Too old for computers? Portland State University, Portland, OR. Retrieved May 2000 from http://web.pdx.edu/~psu01435/tooold.html.

Schofield, J. (1999, June 10). Older hands weave the Web. There's nothing special about being retiring age – except over 65s make up one fifth of the population. *The Guardian*, p. 2.

Sheldon, P. (1993a). Destination Information Systems, *Annals of Tourism Research*, 20, 633-649.

Silverman, D. (2001). *Interpreting Qualitative Data: Methods for Analysing, Talk, Text and Interaction*, 2nd edition. London: Sage.

Statistics Canada (2003). The Daily, August 21, 2001. Retrieved October 2004 from http://www.statcan.ca/Daily/English/010824/d010824b.htm.

Susskind, A.M., Bonn, M.A., & Dev, C. (2003). To look or book: An examination of consumers' apprehensiveness toward Internet use. *Journal of Travel Research*, *41*(3), 256-264.

Szymanski, D.M., & Hise, R.T. (2000). E-satisfaction: An initial examination. *Journal of Retailing*, *76*(3), 309-322.

Tierney, P. (2000). Internet-based evaluation of tourism website effectiveness: Methodological issues and survey results. *Journal of Travel Research*, *39*(2), 212-219.

Trocchia, P.J., & Janda, S. (2000). A phenomenological investigation of Internet usage among older individuals. *Journal of Consumer Marketing*, *17*(7), 605-616.

Veal, A.J. (1997). *Research Methods for Leisure and Tourism: A practical guide, 2nd edition*. London: Prentice Hall.

Wang, F., Head, M., & Arthur, N. (2002). E-tailing: An analysis of web impacts on the retail market. *Journal of Business Strategies*, *19*(1), 73-93.

Weber, K., & Roehl, W.S. (1999). Profiling people searching for and purchasing travel products on the world wide web. *Journal of Travel Research*, *37*, 291-298.

Zeithaml, V.A., & Gilly, M.C. (1987). Characteristics affecting the acceptance of retailing technologies: a comparison of elderly and non-elderly consumers. *Journal of Retailing*, *63*, 49-68.

The Impact of Tourism in Mexico

Alexander Oliver Leibold Scherer, Fernanda Valcarcel,
Maité Soto, Juan Carlos Gallego, Alfredo Buenrostro

Tourism is the most important tool that a country has to convey its history, traditions, culture, to name but a few, to the world.

For Mexico, tourism is already a major source of income but it could well become the most important if the people and the government were more willing to work at it.

Mexico has far more to offer than sun and beaches. There are many divers attractions ranging from colonial and cosmopolitan cities to forests and deserts. Mexico also boasts one of most appealing cuisines in the world and looks back on a long and fascinating history. Additionally the Mexicans are very hospitable and will do their utmost to accommodate the tourists, although this varies from region to region.

If well-managed, tourism could mean a source of income for the many people in need of work, thus ensuring a higher standard of living.

There is a lot of interest in Mexico and what is has to offer and with real commitment from the public and private sectors of the country the impact of tourism could be increased.

We should work hand in hand to ensure that the tourist will talk favorably of our country and want to return. Not just for the sake of the income they generate, but for our own sake.

1. Introduction

The name Mexico, comes from the Náhuatl "Metzlli" (which means moon), and "xictli" (which means navel), combining this, the meaning of the word Mexico in this ancient tongue is "the navel of the moon" named after the great Tenochtitlan which in ancient times was built in the center of Texcoco lake, also known as "Moon Lake".

This is one of the many cultural traditions that our ancestors have passed down to us, as part of one of the most advanced ancient civilizations, evident in along literary tradition, amazing architectural structures, and for their time a very well organized system of commerce, transportation, religion and sports.

Mexico can offer tourism to suit all kind of tastes, far from the cliché depicted in movies. Whether you visit a historic place or stroll through colonial towns you will be astonished at how well preserved and clean everything is. Alexander von Humboldt once said that Mexico city was the city of palaces not because of the actual number of palaces but because the magnificent colonial buildings seemed so palatial.

Business travel is another important source of income. Mexico has a great number of convention centers which have the latest technology and are used by global companies. In Mexico city alone there is an entire area devoted to business tourism where you will find everything that caters to the business traveler's needs.

Those more interested in eco-tourism will find in Mexico a country with huge diversity of flora and fauna. Over 65% of Mexico is made up of forests, jungles and conservation areas. Mexico is home to 10% of the world's flora, ranking fourth place in the world for its diversity of plant species.

The same is true of the animal world. "Cabo Punto" (Cape Point), which is located east from the State of Baja California, was named "The Aquarium of the World", by Jack Cousteau due to its incredible variety of species.

If none of the above appeal to you, you can try the beautiful beaches which, according to studies by the WTO and The federal Tourism Secretary, span over eleven thousand kilometers of coast.

The purpose of this essay is to arouse interest in the reader to explore new territories and experience the wonders of Mexico for himself. Therefore we are going to introduce various aspects of Mexico and show their tourist potential.

2. Tourist Potential

2.1 Beach Resorts

For Mexico these resorts account for the largest number of tourists at national level. The wonderful coastline and the weather fulfill all the expectations tourists may have.

The states Baja California Sur, Colima, Guerrero, Jalisco, Nayarit, Oaxaca, Quintana Roo and Sinaloa have joined forces to improve the destinations and find ways to ensure their sustainable development. We have chosen three resorts to illustrate this.

(1)   Acapulco
Acapulco, currently one of the most important and representative Mexican ports, is the most popular beach destination among young Mexicans and foreigners. Tourist activities include bungee jumping, fishing and water sports, and a lively nightlife.

(2)   Cancún, Isla Mujeres and Playa del Carmen
These are amongst the most frequented destinations on the Riviera Maya lapped by the turquoise waters of the Caribbean Sea.

Cancun has a great nightlife and is an excellent destination for young tourists who enjoy traveling with friends or with a partner.

In Isla Mujeres and Playa del Carmen, tourists can visit archeological sites and beautiful eco touristic parks, such as Xel-Ha and Xcaret, where you can snorkel in underground rivers, go scuba diving on the Great Mayan Reef, or explore the jungle by mountain bike, jeep or on horseback.

(3)   Los Cabos
This is one of the most beautiful and exclusive destinations in Mexico, located at the southern tip of Baja California Sur. During the winter months, tourists can see the arrival of gray whales and their migration route. Activities such as kayaking, diving and fishing can be done the whole year round.

The government, along with the private sector, must find ways to protect and preserve the resources of these regions, for, unless they cooperate, these destinations will be permanently destroyed. The government has drawn up a list of aspects to be considered in order to ensure the image and quality of the resorts.

- The improvement of the image of traditional destinations.
- The improvement of the quality of service for the benefit of the tourist.
- Development of tourism products based on the strategy of differentiation and diversification.
- Regulation of informal commerce.
- Conservation of beaches.

These aspects are aimed at preserving these beach resorts and their various activities, to achieve a balance and guarantee viable development not only through government help, but also through heightened awareness of social responsibility and environmental education.

2.2 The Heart of Mexico

"The Heart of Mexico" is one of the most important regional tourism development projects, which strives to meet the expectations of the present tourists.

This project benefits the industrialists and the service providers by offering great opportunities for investment, growth and development of new businesses. One of the objectives of this project is to position the products and tourist destinations found in the "the heart of Mexico" in national and international markets, in order to maintain and increase levels of competitiveness and profitability. The states on which this project is focused are: Distrito Federal, Estado de Mexico, Guerrero, Hidalgo, Morelos and Tlaxcala.

Distrito federal, (Mexico city)

Mexico City is the largest and most representative city in the entire country, currently with a population of over app. 25 million people. The oldest part of Mexico City, contains some of the country's most cherished cultural treasures. Founded on the ruins of the former Aztec city, its most important buildings are:

- The National Palace,
- the Palace of Fine Arts and
- the Postal Palace.

Santa Fe is one of the newer economic developments in Mexico City; it is one the trendiest zones and is filled with newly built companies and hotels to meet the needs of tourists. The focus here is on business tourism making it a perfect place for conferences and conventions.

In Mexico City you can find all sorts of activities to fill your days with culture and entertainment. Important cultural attractions are: the Azteca Stadium, Xochimilco and all the museums: the Rufino Tamayo Museum, the Anthropology and History National Museum, the Franz Mayer

Museum, the Greater Temple Museum and the fine Arts Museum.

A very important aspect of Mexican culture is the Catholic religion. Since the arrival of the Spaniards, almost 90% of the population have practiced this religion. The Virgin of Guadalupe is the most important religious icon that the Mexican culture has.

The "Heart of Mexico" project serves to promote the increase of both, domestic and foreign tourists while developing the infrastructure of the host communities. As not only Mexico City but also the state of Mexico is involved, another important tourist attraction will be mentioned.

Teotihuacan, a city founded by the Aztec civilization, was a major trading center, and is the archaeological site which attracts the highest number of tourists in the country. The archaeological excavations in Teotihuacan continue until the present days.

2.3 Cortés sea Barrancas del Cobre

The Cortés sea/Copper Canyon project includes states such as Baja California Sur, Sinaloa, Chihuahua and Sonora where the sea, the desert and mountains provide a variety of tourist attractions of incomparable beauty.

This project aims to widen the range of tourist destinations in Mexico. Among the best known destinations and attractions of the program are: Cortès Sea, Copper Canyon, and the tourist train "El Chepe" which connects the cities of Chihuahua and Los Mochis, traversing some of the most spectacular areas of the Copper Canyon, transporting over 260,000 tourists each year.

This tourist circuit is supported by the private sector and government, together with projects such as: Developing new tourism products as well as training and reallocating resources that directly benefit the local program. It will be further developed and aims to attract more tourists every year with improved destinations and service.

The local communities will benefit from these training programs as more jobs will be generated and the quality of life will be improved.

2.4   Mayan World

The "Mayan World" includes the states of Campeche, Chiapas, Quintana Roo, Tabasco and Yucatán, covering an area of 241.784 km².

Among the main objectives is to promote the "Mayan World", through initiatives aimed at developing new products and continually improving the existing ones, at the same time ensuring sustainable development, with the participation of public and private sectors and incorporating local communities.

Thanks to the great legacy that the Mayan civilization left, we can still appreciate all the architectural wonders and their cultural heritage at such Mayan sites as: Tulum, Palenque and Chichén Itzá, which has been elected one of the New Seven Wonders of the World.

The "Mayan World"-project was created in order to combine government and private sector efforts to support the recovery of archaeological sites, positioning the brand "Mayan World" at national and international fairs, and thereby seeking support from international agents.

2.5   Magic Towns

The "Magic Town"-project involves promoting towns in Mexico which comply with certain requirements, such as town conservation, level of cleanliness, cultural and historical value, among others.

One of the main objectives of this regional plan is to highlight the attraction of the locations in the interior of the country, ranging from adventure tourism to ecotourism to culture tourism.

This plan is called "Magic Towns", precisely because of the magic that emanates from the towns involved and the indigenous people and their history. History comes alive in the participating towns of: Huasca de Campo, Pátzcuaro, Real de Catorce, San Cristóbal de las Casas, Taxco, Tequila and Valle de Bravo

2.6   Route of the Gods

This project covers the main cities which were founded in prehistoric times along the coast of the Golf of Mexico, to the Pacific Ocean, going through the States of Oaxaca, Puebla, Tlaxcala, Veracruz, and Mexico City.

The main objective of the plan is to market destinations of historical and cultural value. Obviously the main attraction is cultural tourism; this also includes business, beach holidays and alternative tourism. This project started 2001 with the purpose of showing the world how extensive and fascinating Mexican history is.

The project includes the development of products to facilitate the economic growth of the region, such as providing the necessary infrastructure and improving the utilities of the urban region in order to make the tourists' stay more comfortable. This plan encourages private investment to a point but it is strictly controlled by the government to ensure the protection of the local communities.

To illustrate the influence of Mexican history, ancient civilizations such as the Aztecas, Mayas, Nahuas, Totonacs, Zapotecos and Mixtecos were included in this project. The Zapotecos for example were responsible for the invention of ball games, the Totonacs are known for their Voladores, who perform a special fertility dance, hanging upside down from a pole.

2.7 Colonial treasures

Mexico is the perfect destination to travel through time, with a great variety of destinations, famous monuments and a complete journey through history.

Few places boast such patrimonial and historical wealth; in an environment full of natural beauty and a wide selection of activities, making these places touristic products covering different aspects such as culture, business and alternative tourism.

Hidden in the heart of this beautiful country, you can find amazing cities where time has been frozen; these cities, known as Colonial Treasures, are part of a new project of the same name aiming to explore and show another side of Mexico, including its folklore, history, and amazing countryside. These places will give each visitor an unparalleled experience.

The Colonial Treasures project includes the states of Aguascalientes, Durango, Guanajuato, Michoacan, Queretaro, San Luis Potosi and Zacatecas; it is attracting mostly national tourists, but also increasingly American and European tourism. Each city has different and unique attractions, illustrating the country's history. The colonial period was a fundamental part of Mexico´s evolution, and defines what this country is today.

(1) Aguascalientes

The historic city of Aguascalientes, capital of the state bearing the same name, is located in northern-central region of Mexico 504 miles, from Mexico City and 130km from Zacatecas. Aguascalientes is defined as an attractive and versatile town having very good transport links and a wide range of attractions, some of which include: the Government Palace, with its elaborate murals, the Plaza de la Patria, the Cathedral Basilica of Nuestra Señora de la Asunción, and the Templo de San Antonio.

(2) Guanajuato

Located in the heart of the southern plateau crossed by small mountain ranges, the state of Guanajuato has tiered floor vast plains ideal for cultivation, known as the Bajio. Its art-festivals are nationally and internationally reknown.

Guanajuato, a former mining town with a rich history, has a bohemian atmosphere which is created by its architecture, together with its squares, alleys and underground tunnels. These all serve to make it an unforgettable experience for the visitor. Guanajuato is a natural stage of artistic events with several museums and galleries. Some of the other colonial attractions include:

The Basilica de Nuestra Señora de Guanajuato, the Santuario de Cristo Rey, the Museo Diego Rivera, the Callejón del Beso, the Teatro Juárez, the Monumento a El Pípila, the Iconography of Don Quixote and the Living Museum of the Legends.

(3) Queretaro

Fertile valleys, canyons and plains characterize the state of Queretaro. Located in the central region of the Republic, in the Panuco River basin, it is halfway between Mexico City and the states of Guanajuato and Michoacan. The state capital of the same name is located in the southwest of the territory.

The history of the capital city is preserved by its churches, monuments and Adocreto streets, paved with pink stone. The beautiful historic center of Queretaro has been declared by UNESCO as Cultural Patrimony of Humanity. In contrast it is also a city with dynamic growth, modern infrastructure, broad avenues, big shopping malls and impressive industrial zones.

Some of the colonial attractions include: The Templo de Santa Clara, the Templo de San Agustin, the Temple and ex-Convent of San Francisco, the Antiguo Convento de San Jose de Gracia and Temple Capuchi, the Theater of the Republic and the Auditorium Josefa Ortiz de Domínguez.

(4)   San Luis Potosi

North of the central highlands of the Republic, between the Sierra Madre Oriental, called Potosina Huasteca, and the mountains of Zacatecas, is the state of San Luis Potosi. In colonial times this was a province with abundant mineral wealth which filled the coffers of the Spanish crown.

Called the "City of Gardens" for its many plazas, the state capital covers an arid plain. Among its many monuments are the Aranzazu Chapel, the Cathedral of San Luis Rey and the San Francisco Church. The city has also important museums: the National Museum of the Mask that showcases more than 700 indigenous religious masks; Potosi Regional Museum which displays artifacts in the Huasteca and Folk Art Museum, among others.

(5)   Zacatecas

The most important mining state is characterized by mountainous desert landscape, rocky hills, deep canyons and barren plains. This region is famous for its table wines which are becoming increasingly prestigious, as well as for the traditional drink of mescal. This regions trademark is its silver jewelry inlaid with gold and semi-precious stones.

The city of Zacatecas is located on the slopes of Cerro de la Bufa and is a magnificent historical monument of the colonial era. Its streets, squares and alleys, rich in history and architecture, are testimony to the colonial era of colonization when Zacatecas became one of the major cities of the region thanks to its thriving mines.

The colonial attractions include some excellent museums such the Museo Pedro Coronel, the Francisco Goitia Museum and the Museo Rafael Coronel. The ex-convent of Guadalupe, an old colonial building which was an important center of evangelization is located just minutes from Zacatecas and is one of the most important Franciscan buildings of the eighteenth century. Worth visiting is the museum which houses a fine collection of colonial paintings including works by major Mexican artists as: Cristóbal de Villalpando, Andres Lopez, Nicolas Rodriguez Juarez, Ibarra, Gabriel José de Ovalle, Antonio de Torres and Miguel Cabrera.

(6) Durango

The City of Durango with its splendid historic center is a must-see for visitors. This historic center is the eighth largest in the country and is considered one of the most beautiful.

Durango's attractions are many and varied: it has two biosphere reserves, with abundant wildlife including over 250 species of migratory and endemic birds. It has architectural gems and archaeological sites, such as cave paintings.

These are places that will never be forgotten, places which will leave lasting impressions of the natural beauty and cultural wealth of our country.

3. Conclusions

Mexico boasts such a wide variety of destinations, offering so many impressive attractions, that the tourist can have a different experience each time he visits.

The country is famous worldwide for its natural reserves, including beaches, forests, mountains and volcanoes and the various projects aim to insure that eco-tourism will gain in importance in Mexico.

On the other hand you can visit cosmopolitan Mexico City, one of the biggest cities in the world yet still preserving its historic charm. If you want to experience the magic of Mexico there are always the magic towns where the mysticism and traditions are kept alive.

For business travelers Mexico offers state of the art convention centers with the latest technology ensuring your business event will be a complete success.

However, Mexico is first and foremost its people. It is our responsibility to make each visit a memorable experience for the tourist, while at the same time contributing to the upkeep of our heritage.

Hollywood has painted a picture of Mexico as a country full of ignorant people, promoting the cliché of the "charro", a person never seen without his sombrero, a donkey and a bottle full of mescal, living in an ugly one-horse-town surrounded by nopales.

Having read this article you will find that Mexico is so much more: It will provide unforgettable experiences beyond your expectations.

References

Enciclopedia Historia de Mexico, Salvat Editores, Mexico, 1978.

MAGAÑA, Patricia. VILLASEÑOR, José Luis. "La Flora de Mexico", CIENCIAS, núm. 66, UNAM, Mexico, Junio de 2002.

COLL-HURTADO Atlántida. "Nuevo Atlas Nacional de Mexico", Recopilado por el Instituto de Geografía, Universidad Nacional Autónoma de Mexico, 2007.

Further Information

United Nations Educational, Scientific and Cultural Organization (www.unesco.org)

World Tourism Organization (www.unwto.org)

Explorando Mexico (www.explorandomexico.com)

Comisión Nacional Forestal (www.conafor.gob.mx)

Secretaría de Medio Ambiente y Recursos Naturales (www.semarnat.gob.mx)

Instituto Nacional de Geografía y Estadística (www.inegi.gob.mx)

Secretaría de Turismo (www.sectur.gob.mx)

Huasca de Campo (www.huascapueblomagico.gob.mx)

Pátzcuaro (www.patzcuaro.com)

Real de Catorce (www.realdecatorce.net)

San Cristobal de las Casas (www.sancristobal.gob.mx)

Taxco (www.taxco.gob.mx)

Valle de Bravo (www.valledebravo.gob.mx)

Aguascalientes (www.aguascalientes.gob.mx)

Durango (www.durango.gob.mx)

Guanajuato (www.guanajuato.gob.mx)

Michoacán (www.michoacan.gob.mx)

Querétaro(www.queretaro.gob.mx)

Zacatecas (www.zacatecas.gob.mx)

Abbreviation

ANOVA	Analysis of Variance
ATLAS	Association for Tourism and Leisure Education
BTM	Berlin Tourism Marketing GmbH
DestiMon	Destination-Monitor
Est.	Established
FIFA	Fédération Internationale de Football Association
GDP	Gross Domestic Product
GIS	Geographic Information Systems
ICNT	International Competence Network of Tourism
ICOM	International Council of Museums
IMT	Institut für Management und Tourismus
ITB	Icelandic Tourism Board
ITC	International Tourism Conference
NORCE	Northern Coastal Experience
NTS	Nordsee-Tourismus-Service GmbH
PAGIS	Participatory Approach Using Geographical Information Systems
UNESCO	United Nations Educational, Scientific and Cultural Organization
UNWTO	United Nations World Tourism Organisation
WTM	World Travel Monitor
WTO	World Tourism Organisation

About the Authors

Alfredo Buenrostro, *Student of the Bachelor Degree for Tourism Management.*

Prof. Dr. Bernd Eisenstein, *born on the 20th of August 1965, completed his Dipl.-Kaufmann and Dipl.-Geograph at Trier University where he did his doctorate supervised by Prof. Christoph Becker as well. Since 1997 he has had a position as Professor for International Tourism Management at Westcoast University of Applied Sciences in Heide/Holstein and since 2006 he has been director of the Institut für Management und Tourismus (IMT) of Westcoast University of Applied Sciences. Prof. Bernd Eisenstein collected further lecturing experiences at Trier University and University of Applied Sciences Worms and, has conducted and co-ordinated numerous consultancy and research projects, in particular concerning destination management, tourism demand and strategic tourism management.*

Juan Carlos Gallego, *Student of the Bachelor Degree for Tourism Management.*

Dr. Alice Gräupl, *completed her Bachelor of Arts (Hons) in Tourism (1999) and Master of Arts in Tourism Management (2000) at the University of Derby, UK. Shortly afterwards she continued her studies by enrolling in the Ph.D. programme at the same university. Her doctorate was awarded in June 2008. Since January 2005, Alice has been working as a Lecturer at AUT University in Auckland, New Zealand. Her research areas are Tourism and ICTs, with particular focus on the Internet as an online information search tool.*

Dr. Edward H. Huijbens, *finished a B.Sc. in Geography at the University of Iceland in the spring 2000. Prior to that he got his Iceland Tourist Guide certificate in 1998. After completing his B.Sc. he moved to England and completed his MA, late in 2001 and later a PhD in Cultural Geography 2006, both at Durham University. From 2004 to 2006, along with completing the PhD, he taught and did research at the University of Iceland, both in the faculty of science and the faculty of economics and business administration. He assumed directorship of the Icelandic Tourism Research Centre in the summer of 2006. Edward is the author of articles in several scholarly journals in both Iceland and internationally and has co-edited Technology in Society/Society in Technology (2005, University of Iceland Press), Sensi/able Spaces: Space, art and the environment (2007, Cambridge Scholars Press) Contact: Edward@unak.is*

Dr. John S. Hull *is currently Associate Professor at Thompson Rivers University's Tourism Management Programme in British Columbia, Canada. He is also a member of the New Zealand Tourism Research Institute, New Zealand, and a guest professor at the Icelandic Tourism Research Centre, Iceland. He completed his PhD in tourism geography at McGill University, Canada where his research examined the sustainability of tourism around some of the oldest seabird sanctuaries in North America. His present research addresses sustainable tourism, strategic tourism planning and destination development, culinary tourism, the greening of tourism, business development, as well as spa and wellness planning for the hospitality and tourism industry. John has consulted on projects in North America, Europe, the Middle East, South America, Africa, and Asia. Contact: jhull@tru.ca*

Alexander Koch, *born on the 6th of February 1984, completed his Bachelor of Business Administration (BBA hons) in Leisure and Tourism Management at University of Applied Sciences Stralsund in 2009 with distinction. Since 2009 he has been employed as a member of the project team of the Institut für Management und Tourismus (IMT) of Westcoast University of Applied Sciences in the fields of market research and consultancy.*

Charyn López, *is currently teacher in the Bachelor Degree for Gastronomy and Tourism Management. She specializes in the culinary culture of Mexico. She also has completed a Master degree in marketing and publicity.*

Dr. Michael Lück, *currently holds the position of Associate Professor in the School of Hospitality and Tourism, AUT University in Auckland, New Zealand. He is Head of the Tourism & Events department, and an Associate Director of the New Zealand Tourism Research Institute (NZTRI), where he is responsible for the marine tourism research programme area (together with Professor Mark Orams). Michael's primary research interests are in the wider area of marine tourism, with a focus on marine wildlife tourism and interpretation and education. He is also interested in ecotourism, sustainable tourism, the impacts of tourism, aviation, and gay tourism. Michael has developed a keen interest in innovative and alternative teaching and assessment methods. He has published in international academic journals, and contributed to various books. He is the overall editor or co-editor of six books, the Encyclopedia of Tourism and Recreation in Marine Environments (CABI), the founding editor of the academic journal Tourism in Marine Environments, and Associate Editor of the Journal of Ecotourism.*

Mtro. Alexander Oliver Leibold Scherer, *is currently the coordinator of the Bachelor of Gastronomy. He is also coordinator of professional practice and representative for Social Activities at the University. He completed a master's degree in marketing and publicity, and now is studying a PhD in Innovation and social responsibility. He also wrote a book "Customer and service quality" and participates with different magazines as an co-autor with other teachers to write articles.*

Elmarie Slabbert, *is an associate professor at North-West University (Potchefstroom Campus). She specialises in the social impact of tourism, tourism marketing communication, event management and tourism management. She is currently one of the senior researchers in the School of Business Management and the Niche for the Socio-Economic impact of Tourism which focuses on various aspects of tourism management. She is referee for the National Research Foundation (NRF), the Southern Africa Business Review and the South African Journal for Research in Sport, Physical Education and Recreation. After completion of her PhD she focused on acquiring research funds awarded to her by the National Research Foundation for analysing the social impact of events in South Africa (2007-2010). From 2005 19 of her post-graduate students completed their studies with success. Currently she is the supervisor of 4 Master's degree, 8 MTech and 4 PhD students. She is an external promoter for the MTech*

Students at the Vaal University of Technology. At international level she has presented 22 papers at international conferences. Prof Slabbert has also presented 6 papers at national conferences, written (with other authors or as sole author) 3 books, 10 chapters in books, 10 accredited articles and 47 research reports.

Maité Soto, *Student of the Bachelor Degree for Tourism Management.*

Fernanda Valcarcel, *Student of the Bachelor Degree for Tourism Management.*

Peet van der Merwe: *Petrus van der Merwe is currently a senior lecturer in tourism management at North West University: Potchefstroom Campus. As researcher he also forms part of the NRF research niche namely SEIT (Socio-economic Impact of Tourism). Petrus obtained his degree in 1994, honours degree in 1995 and master's degree in 1999 from the previous known Department of Recreation and Tourism. Petrus completed his PhD (2004) in tourism management and in 2010 became a associate professor. His field of expertise lies in game farm tourism and ecotourism. Research output are as follows: Peer reviewed articles (13), Articles in process of reviewing (5), Popular articles (14), Projects (19), Research reports (16), Books (1), Chapters (2), Completed masters (4), masters in process (6), PhD students in process (3), International conferences (17), National conferences (6) and International quest lectures (2).*

Dipl.-Ing. Anja Wollesen *is born on the 30 of March 1968, completed her Dipl.-Landsape Planning at Technical University of Berlin in 1994. She has been employed for 15 years as senior consultant of tourism Management and regional development, before she started as scientific collaborator in the project team of the Institut für Management und Tourismus (IMT) of Westcoast University of Applied Sciences in the fields of Destination Management and culture tourism. Her current research focus is the strategic control of culture and leisure facilities to sustainable securing as cultural infrastructure in rural areas. Anja Wollesen is also teaching destination management and leisure and event management at the Westcoast University of Applied Sciences.*

Acknowledgements

The editors wish to thank all authors for their hard work and their willingness to polish their presentations held originally during the two successful conferences hosted by the University Anáhuac (Mexico) and the North West University (South Africa) respectively for this publication. The book could neither have been published without their cooperation nor without the help of Anke Becker, Ciara Colgan-Buchenau and Dörte Renken, in editing the translations and helping with all the technical details which need attention with any publication. Finally the editors have to acknowledge the long-term commitment of Martin Meidenbauer Verlag, Munich, towards the series Schriftenreihe des IMT, of which this volume is the fifth installment.

Christian Eilzer
Bernd Eisenstein
Wolfgang Georg Arlt

Institut für Management und Tourismus der FH Westküste

Das Institut für Management und Tourismus (IMT) ist seit Juni 2006 als In-Institut an der Fachhochschule Westküste angesiedelt. Unter dem Dach des Instituts werden sämtliche Hochschulaktivitäten in den Feldern betriebswirtschaftlich orientierter Tourismusforschung, -qualifizierung und -beratung gebündelt und miteinander vernetzt. Großer Wert wird dabei auf Unabhängigkeit der Forschung, Nähe zur Praxis und wissenschaftliche Fundierung gelegt.

Das IMT entstand im Rahmen des Projektes „Aufbau eines Kompetenzzentrums für betriebswirtschaftliche Tourismusforschung und -qualifizierung". Gefördert wurde dieses Projekt aus Mitteln des Europäischen Sozialfonds und des Innovationsfonds Schleswig-Holstein. Weitere Unterstützung erhielt das Kompetenzzentrum durch finanzielle Zuschüsse weiterer Partner und durch einen Projektbeirat mit Akteuren aus Wirtschaft, Wissenschaft und Politik.

Das Kompetenzzentrum verfolgt als zentraler Bestandteil des Bildungs-, Beratungs- und Forschungsschwerpunktes Tourismus der Fachhochschule Westküste die Zielsetzung, die wissenschaftliche Weiterbildung und Qualifizierung im Tourismus zu fördern sowie u. a. über anwendungsorientierte Forschungsprojekte den Wissenstransfer zwischen Hochschule und Wirtschaft zu intensivieren. Dazu greift das IMT praxisrelevante Fragestellungen auf und bearbeitet diese gemeinsam mit Akteuren der Wirtschaft zum Nutzen der beteiligten Projektpartner.

Weitere Informationen zum IMT unter www.imt-fhw.de.

Besucherleitsysteme

Entwicklung und Anwendung eines Instruments zu ihrer Bewertung –
Dargestellt am Beispiel des Biosphärenreservats Rhön
(Schriftenreihe des Instituts für Management und Tourismus 1)
Von Christian Eilzer
2007, 197 Seiten, Paperback, Euro 29,90/CHF 51,00, ISBN 978-3-89975-095-9

Basisinfrastruktur, Marketingtool, Profilierungsinstrument – Besucherleitsysteme sind ein wichtiger Bestandteil des Angebotsbündels einer Destination. Wanderleitsysteme, Besucherinformationspunkte oder Hotelleitsysteme sind für Touristen in einer ihnen weniger vertrauten Umgebung bedeutsame Orientierungshilfen, etwa zum Auffinden nachgefragter Ziele. Leiteinrichtungen wie ein verlässliches und informatives Wanderleitsystem tragen zur Erhöhung der Angebotsqualität bei und eröffnen Chancen der Profilierung gegenüber Konkurrenzdestinationen.

Im Fokus dieses Buches steht die Entwicklung einer Methodik zur Bewertung und Optimierung von Leiteinrichtungen sowie deren Anwendung am Beispiel des Biosphärenreservats Rhön. In Sinne einer ganzheitlichen Herangehensweise legt Christian Eilzer dabei ein Verständnis des Begriffs „Besucherleitsystem" zugrunde, das über eine eng gefasste Interpretation der Hinführung, Orientierung und Information durch Beschilderungen hinausgeht. Stattdessen wird das Instrument der Beschilderung mit weiterführenden Maßnahmen der Lenkung und Information verknüpft.

Qualität und Qualifizierung im Tourismus

Anforderungen an ein ganzheitliches Qualitäts- und
Qualifizierungssystem in einer Destination
(Schriftenreihe des Instituts für Management und Tourismus 2)
Von Manon Eckhoff
2007, 166 Seiten, Paperback, Euro 29,90/CHF 53,50, ISBN 978-3-89975-111-6

Die Betonung der Qualität – insbesondere in der Dienstleistung – ist für Destinationen ein zentraler Erfolgsfaktor im touristischen Wettbewerb. Damit steigen auch die Ansprüche an die Qualifikation der Akteure.

Im Mittelpunkt dieses Buches steht die Ableitung der Anforderungen an ein ganzheitliches Qualitäts- und Qualifizierungssystem für Destinationen. Die Autorin formuliert konzeptionelle Leitlinien für die Entwicklung eines Systemansatzes zur Optimierung der touristischen Angebotsqualität. Im Sinne einer ganzheitlichen, interdisziplinären Herangehensweise berücksichtigt dieser in umfassender Weise die Bedeutung des Qualifizierungsaspektes für ein nachhaltiges Qualitätsmanagement.

National Parks and Tourism

Answers to a Global Question from the International Competence
Network of Tourism Management (ICNT)
(Schriftenreihe des Instituts für Management und Tourismus 3)
Hg. von Christian Eilzer/Bernd Eisenstein/Wolfgang Georg Arlt
2008, 186 Seiten, Paperback, Euro 29,90/CHF 53,50, ISBN 978-3-89975-140-6

Der Tourismus ist in Gebieten mit Nationalparks und weiteren geschützten
Landschaften häufig ein wichtiger Wirtschaftsfaktor. Insbesondere in Reisezie-
len mit Schutzgebieten treffen touristische jedoch auch auf naturschützerische
Interessen, die es miteinander zu vereinbaren gilt.

In Beiträgen von Tourismusexperten aus Australien, China, Deutschland, Mexiko und Neuseeland stellt dieses Buch Untersuchungsergebnisse und Fallbei-
spiele aus der Praxis vor. Im Fokus stehen neben den Herausforderungen einer
touristischen Nutzung u. a. Fragen der touristischen Vermarktung oder landes-
typische Besonderheiten.

COTRI Yearbook 2010

China's Outbound Tourism Development
Foreword by Taleb Rifai, Secretary-General UNWTO
(Schriftenreihe des Instituts für Management und Tourismus 4)
Hg. von Wolfgang Georg Arlt
2010, 156 Seiten, Paperback, Euro 24,90/CHF 45,00, ISBN 978-3-89975-191-8

„Das COTRI Yearbook 2010 bietet eine Vielfalt an Artikeln von ausgewiesenen
Wissenschaftlern und Tourismus-Experten aus China und aus anderen Ländern. Leser können neue Erkenntnisse über die Entwicklung des Outbound-
Tourismus aus China in so unterschiedlichen Ländern wie Belgien, Deutschland, Jamaica und Mexiko gewinnen.

Sie finden weiterhin praktische Informationen darüber, wie man die Qualität
touristischer Dienstleistungen zielgerichtet für die spezifischen Bedürfnisse
der chinesischen Reisenden verbessert. Die Vielfältigkeit der im Yearbook ent-
haltenen Informationen läßt mich sicher sein, dass es auf großes Interesse sto-
ßen wird. Schließlich kann der chinesische Outbound-Tourismus von keinem
wichtigen Akteur im Welttourismus-Markt ignoriert werden."

Aus dem Vorwort von Taleb Rifai, Generalsekretär der UNWTO

Ihr Wissenschaftsverlag. Kompetent und unabhängig.

Martin Meidenbauer »

Verlagsbuchhandlung GmbH & Co. KG
Schwanthalerstr. 81 • 80336 München
Tel. (089) 20 23 86 -03 • Fax -04
info@m-verlag.net • www.m-verlag.net